# Patterns of Joint Actions

# Patterns of Joint Actions

AN OUTLINE OF THE FUNDAMENTALS
OF SOCIAL INTERACTION

• • •

*Kenneth Garverick*

© Copyright 2016 Kenneth Garverick
All rights reserved.

ISBN-13: 9781539802860
ISBN-10: 1539802868
Library of Congress Control Number: 2016918209
CreateSpace Independent Publishing Platform
North Charleston, South Carolina

# Contents

Introduction · · · · · · · · · · · · · · · · · · · · · · · · · · · · · · · · · · · · · · ·ix

Part I · · · · · · · · · · · · · · · · · · · · · · · · · · · · · · · · · · · · · · · · · · 1

Chapter 1   Preliminaries - Thinking, Decision Making, and
the Rational Act · · · · · · · · · · · · · · · · · · · · · · · · · · · 3

Thinking · · · · · · · · · · · · · · · · · · · · · · · · · · · · · · · · · 3

   Thought Precedes Action · · · · · · · · · · · · · · · · · 3

   Objects · · · · · · · · · · · · · · · · · · · · · · · · · · · · · 4

   Making Associations Between Objects - Sentences · · · 4

   Sets · · · · · · · · · · · · · · · · · · · · · · · · · · · · · · · 5

   Logical Conclusions and Predictions · · · · · · · · · · · · 6

Decision Making · · · · · · · · · · · · · · · · · · · · · · · · · · · 7

   The Self · · · · · · · · · · · · · · · · · · · · · · · · · · · · · 7

   Goals · · · · · · · · · · · · · · · · · · · · · · · · · · · · · · · 7

The Rational Act · · · · · · · · · · · · · · · · · · · · · · · · · · · 8

   Behavior as Separate, Individual Actions · · · · · · · · · · 8

   The Nine Steps of the Rational Act · · · · · · · · · · · · · 9

Sensitizing Concepts · · · · · · · · · · · · · · · · · · · · · · · · 10

Chapter 2   The Joint Action · · · · · · · · · · · · · · · · · · · · · · · · · 12

Herbert Blumer's Joint Action · · · · · · · · · · · · · · · · · · 12

Boundaries · · · · · · · · · · · · · · · · · · · · · · · · · · · · · · · 13

Common Understandings. · · · · · · · · · · · · · · · · · · · · · 13

| | | |
|---|---|---|
| | Language · · · · · · · · · · · · · · · · · · · · · · · · · · · · · · · · · · | 14 |
| | "Facts" · · · · · · · · · · · · · · · · · · · · · · · · · · · · · · · · · · · | 14 |
| | Situational Common Understandings - The Plan · · · | 14 |
| | Consensus · · · · · · · · · · · · · · · · · · · · · · · · · · · · · · · · · | 15 |
| | Communication · · · · · · · · · · · · · · · · · · · · · · · · · · · · · · | 16 |
| | Blumer's Symbolic Interaction: Definition and Interpretation · · · · · · · · · · · · · · · · · · · · · · · · · · | 16 |
| | Fixed vs. Fluid Common Understandings · · · · · · · · | 17 |
| | Communication and Relationships · · · · · · · · · · · · · | 17 |
| | Similarities vs. Differences with Others · · · · · · · · · | 17 |
| | The Self · · · · · · · · · · · · · · · · · · · · · · · · · · · · · · · · · · · · | 19 |
| | Situational Selves · · · · · · · · · · · · · · · · · · · · · · · · · · · | 19 |
| | The Looking Glass Self · · · · · · · · · · · · · · · · · · · · · · | 20 |
| | Presentation of Self · · · · · · · · · · · · · · · · · · · · · · · · | 21 |
| | Motivation and Self Realization · · · · · · · · · · · · · · · | 22 |
| | Task Completion · · · · · · · · · · · · · · · · · · · · · · · · · · | 23 |
| | Relationship Fulfillment · · · · · · · · · · · · · · · · · · · | 24 |
| Chapter 3 | Patterns of Joint Actions · · · · · · · · · · · · · · · · · · · · · | 29 |
| | Routines · · · · · · · · · · · · · · · · · · · · · · · · · · · · · · · · · · · | 29 |
| | Careers · · · · · · · · · · · · · · · · · · · · · · · · · · · · · · · · · · · · | 31 |
| | Social Groups · · · · · · · · · · · · · · · · · · · · · · · · · · · · · · · | 33 |
| | Links and Networks · · · · · · · · · · · · · · · · · · · · · · · · · · | 35 |
| | The Circulation of Elites and The Military Industrial Complex · · · · · · · · · · · · · · · · · · · · · · · · · · · | 37 |
| | Social Conflict · · · · · · · · · · · · · · · · · · · · · · · · · · · · · · | 37 |
| Chapter 4 | Five Factors · · · · · · · · · · · · · · · · · · · · · · · · · · · · · · · · · | 40 |
| | Physiological and Psychological Needs · · · · · · · · · · · | 40 |
| | Values · · · · · · · · · · · · · · · · · · · · · · · · · · · · · · · · · · · · · | 41 |
| | Status and Conspicuous Consumption · · · · · · · · · · · | 47 |
| | The Law of Diminishing Returns · · · · · · · · · · · · · · · | 51 |
| | Saving Face · · · · · · · · · · · · · · · · · · · · · · · · · · · · · · · · | 53 |
| Chapter 5 | Types of Joint Actions · · · · · · · · · · · · · · · · · · · · · · · | 56 |
| | Teamwork · · · · · · · · · · · · · · · · · · · · · · · · · · · · · · · · · · | 57 |

|  |  |  |
|---|---|---|
| | Contracts | 59 |
| | Competition and Conflict | 61 |
| | Sociable Interaction | 62 |
| | Play | 64 |

| | | |
|---|---|---|
| Part II | | 67 |
| Chapter 6 | An Alternative Paradigm: Joint Actions and the Study of Social Groups | 69 |
| | Social Structures and Social Aggregates | 69 |
| | Joint Actions and Studying Structures | 71 |
| | Joint Actions and Studying Aggregates | 73 |
| Chapter 7 | Cause and Effect | 75 |
| | Primary Causes: Making Rational Decisions | 77 |
| | Secondary Causes: Conditions, Factors, and Events Affecting Joint Actions | 78 |
| | History | 80 |
| | Making Predictions | 82 |
| Chapter 8 | Methods and Macro Sociology | 85 |
| | Six Questions: Who, What, When, Where How, and Why | 86 |
| | Methods | 87 |
| | Participant Observation | 87 |
| | Video and Audio Records | 88 |
| | Interviews and Histories | 88 |
| | Surveys and Polls | 89 |
| | Statistics | 90 |
| | Interactionism and the Study of Macro-Social Phenomena | 91 |
| | *The Protestant Ethic and the Spirit of Capitalism* Revisited | 93 |
| Chapter 9 | Social Change | 95 |
| | Change as Inevitable | 95 |
| | Defining *Social* Change | 96 |

Sources of Change · · · · · · · · · · · · · · · · · · · · · · · · · · · · 97
    Environmental Change · · · · · · · · · · · · · · · · · · · · · 97
    Innovation and Imitation· · · · · · · · · · · · · · · · · · · · · 97
    Large Organizations · · · · · · · · · · · · · · · · · · · · · · · 98
    Widespread Failure in Patterns of Joint Actions · · · · 99
    Changes in Common Understandings · · · · · · · · · · · 99
Predicting the Weather.· · · · · · · · · · · · · · · · · · · · · · · · 105

**Chapter 10**   Other Concepts · · · · · · · · · · · · · · · · · · · · · · · · · 108
Authority and Leadership · · · · · · · · · · · · · · · · · · · · · · 109
Community · · · · · · · · · · · · · · · · · · · · · · · · · · · · · · · · 110
Culture · · · · · · · · · · · · · · · · · · · · · · · · · · · · · · · · · · · 111
Collective Behavior · · · · · · · · · · · · · · · · · · · · · · · · · · 113
Personal Networking· · · · · · · · · · · · · · · · · · · · · · · · · · 113
"Selflessness" · · · · · · · · · · · · · · · · · · · · · · · · · · · · · · 114

Conclusion - Applications · · · · · · · · · · · · · · · · · · · · · · 117
References· · · · · · · · · · · · · · · · · · · · · · · · · · · · · · · · · 119

# Introduction

● ● ●

THIS BOOK'S PURPOSE AND DIRECTION stem from three premises. The first is that human beings are profoundly *social* beings. Everything we do is either a part of social interaction or is influenced by social interaction. This is one of the most defining characteristics of our species and is the primary reason sociology exists as an academic discipline. If we want to understand ourselves and what we do, understanding the process of social interaction is a worthwhile and, indeed, necessary endeavor.

The second premise is that, as this book's subtitle suggests, there are relatively few fundamental properties of social interaction. Certainly, social interaction can take on many forms and is often extremely complex and problematic. However, when people interact with one another, regardless of their language, culture, or customs, the process always incorporates a handful of basic principles. There are a finite set of truths which apply to *all* social interaction. The purpose of this book is to examine these fundamental truths.

The third premise is a simple but highly significant observation noted by Herbert Blumer in his essay *Sociological Implications of the Thought of George Herbert Mead* (1966). Blumer (and, indirectly, Mead) made many worthwhile observations in this essay, but perhaps the most important one (at least for this book's purpose) was that social interaction does not occur in a seamless flow. When people interact, they do so by engaging in separate and distinct *joint* actions. These are units of social interaction in which two or more people perform actions in concert, or jointly, with one another - hence the phrase *joint actions*. These joint actions are the basic units of social interaction.

Recognizing that the joint action is the basic unit of social interaction provides direction to the study of social interaction. Blumer noted that all joint actions have certain fundamental and universal properties. The best way, then, to begin a study of social interaction is to examine and expand upon these fundamental properties of joint actions. That is, just as chemistry students begin by studying the basic nature of atoms and molecules - the elemental units of all matter - it is logical to begin the study of social interaction by studying the basic nature of joint actions. This is the aim of the first two chapters of this book.

After examining the universal properties of joint actions, three questions, and areas of study, naturally come to mind. First of all, people do not engage in joint actions in a haphazard manner. They engage in *patterns* of joint actions. It is therefore interesting and useful to look at how, and why, people engage in different patterns of joint activity. Secondly, it is natural to question what general *factors* affect joint activity. And thirdly, we may question how may we can logically separate joint actions into different *types* of joint actions. Chapters three through five address these questions.

Part II of this book deals with the question of how the study of joint actions fits within the broader field of sociology. Sociologists address a wide range of issues, so it is worthwhile, I believe, to discuss how our knowledge of joint actions may be of use in studying these various areas of interest. The topics covered include: how the study of joint actions compares to and aids the study of social groups (Chapter Six), the issue of cause and effect (Chapter Seven), the processes of research and analysis (Chapter Eight), and social change and predictability (Chapter Nine). Finally, Chapter Ten presents a few examples of how focusing on the processes of joint activity may alter our view of a few of the more conventional topics in sociology. Mead and Blumer laid a firm foundation of concepts which, I believe, may be applied to all areas of sociological inquiry. The following book endeavors to build upon this foundation.

# Part I

• • •

CHAPTER 1

# Preliminaries - Thinking, Decision Making, and the Rational Act

● ● ●

As mentioned in the Introduction, this book is inspired, in part, by Herbert Blumer's *Sociological Implications of the Thought of George Herbert Mead* (1966). Much of this chapter and the next cites and builds on this work.

## Thinking

Human beings think, and they have the capacity to remember. This, more than anything else, is what sets us apart from other animals and makes us "human". Thought and Action are subjects which can be, and have been, discussed in volumes by philosophers and psychologists; but there are a few characteristics of thought and action that are of particular importance to the study of social interaction. These characteristics are as follows:

**Thought precedes action.** This is an obvious enough statement, but its significance is often lost in the study of human behavior. If you consider what "causes" someone to act in a particular way, the most immediate answer is that the person *decided* to act that way. Understanding someone's behavior necessarily involves some appreciation of what that person was thinking prior to the behavior in question. This fact is often ignored or sidestepped by people studying and explaining human behavior. Too often the causes of behavior are directly attributed to some outside influence, such as poverty, the media, or social pressures, without appreciating the role that thinking and decision making has in the process of action. Any thorough understanding of someone's behavior involves some knowledge of what that person was thinking prior to acting.

**Objects.** People think about, and act upon, objects. Since "object" is a term that is central to this discussion, I'll take a moment to define it in the way Blumer defined it in the above mentioned essay. An object is anything that we can refer to. Grammatically speaking, an object is any noun or pronoun. Anything tangible, of course, is an object, such as a house, a person, or a shirt. In addition, anything intangible that we can refer to is also an object, like "space" and "time". Events and actions are objects, such as football games, family dinners, elections, and a walk to the local store. Qualities, such as anger, softness, honesty, and the color red are things we can refer to in the abstract and become objects when we do so. The Federal Government, happiness, justice, astronomy, wars, and peace are all objects because we can refer to them in our thoughts.

Objects have no intrinsic meaning in and of themselves. The meaning of objects lies in the way we act toward them or in the way they affect our actions. A car's importance, for example, lies in our ability to use it to get from point A to point B. A pan is an object we use in cooking - our action toward it gives it its meaning. Honesty is an object we think about when deciding what politician to vote for or when telling a child the proper way to behave.

**Making Associations Between Objects - Sentences.** When we think, we are making associations, or linking, objects together in some way. Remembering is the act of recalling what these associations are. "Mike jogged around the park with his dog." is a thought linking the objects Mike, his dog, the park, and act of jogging. The resulting association, in this case, describes an event (itself an object) that can be remembered.

When considering the act of thinking, it is helpful to again use a grammatical approach. First of all, the medium of our thoughts is language. We assign symbols (words) to the objects we think about. We use these symbols when we think. It is much more efficient to do this than to remember specific sights and sounds and then to make mental associations using those alone. The vocabulary of a language is largely an inventory of the objects that people are aware of, think about, and act on.

Secondly, we think in sentences. A simple thought, for instance, takes the form of a simple sentence. If thinking is the act of making associations between two or more objects, we do so by putting those objects together in sentences. Similarly, just as thinking is the act of making associations between two or more objects, sentences have at least two parts to them - a subject and a predicate. The objects of our thoughts are the nouns and pronouns of our sentences. Complex thoughts and ideas take the form of complex sentences or a series of related sentences. To pick apart an idea, it helps if you are good at picking apart sentences and can see how sentences logically relate to one another. Obtaining a good understanding of the thoughts and actions of a people involves understanding their language - their vocabulary and grammar - since their words and sentences are the medium of their thoughts. This simple fact forms the basis of, and the purpose behind, the study of linguists.

When we make associations between objects, we do so because the objects *exist or occur together* in some way. We often associate objects together describing some action or event. In the example, "Mike jogged around the park with his dog." Mike acted and the objects occurred together describing an event, and this was the basis for the association between the objects. We also make associations between objects when we note that they are separate parts of a larger whole. For example, in the statement, "The car has a six cylinder engine." the person making this statement (or thinking this thought) is noting that the six cylinder engine is a part of the car, the larger whole.

**Sets.** The above example alludes to another important property of objects. Objects typically occur in sets. We use sets when we think. Each object we think about is commonly comprised of a set of smaller parts. The human body is a set of organs and tissue and bone. A court case is comprised of a set legal procedures, and freedom is something that may be divided into a set of more specific freedoms, as in the Bill of Rights. The objects we think about are also usually parts of larger entities. A building is part of a neighborhood, a neighborhood is part of a town, a town is part of a county, etc. We are aware of objects as being either comprised of a set of small objects, part of a set making a larger whole, or both. The *knowledge* that we have and bring to bear when we act is in large measure knowledge of how we arrange objects into sets creating larger wholes. Sets represent a way we organize the objects around us and make sense of them.

**Logical Conclusions and Predictions.** When objects occur together repeatedly, we become able to make logical conclusions and predictions about them. Thus, if we changed the above example to, "Mike jogged around the park with his dog every night this week.", we might predict that Mike will jog around the park again tonight since that event has been occurring repeatedly. Similarly, if we know that a "whole" exists, we can make conclusions and predictions about the existence of its parts. If we know that if a car exists (a properly working one) we can logically conclude that there is an engine (a necessary part of every car) in there somewhere. Turning this idea around a bit, we may make the general statement that *logical conclusions and predictions are based on objects occurring together on a regular basis.*

Since most objects that we observe are similar to other objects that we've observed in the past, we are able to (a) categorize most objects and give them names and (b) predict what these objects - and others like them - will or will not do in different circumstances. For example, if someone shows me a tennis ball, I can first recognize it as a tennis ball from its appearance. Secondly, I can reasonably predict what will happen if someone drops it on a hard surface (it will bounce) because I have seen other tennis balls bounce before. We thus use our ability to recognize and classify (name) objects to predict what particular objects will do or will not do under different circumstances.

To sum up, thinking is a process which, in part, includes (a) observing objects and classifying them, (b) seeing how these objects relate to one another in different situations, (c) remembering what these associations between objects are, and (d) using what we know about objects to predict what will happen in current and future situations. Thinking involves knowing how some objects come together as a set of objects to form a larger whole. What a person knows about objects and how they relate to one another comprises that person's knowledge. People then use that knowledge to predict what will happen under different circumstances in different situations. People thus use their knowledge as they *plan* their behavior and decide the best course of action to take in a given situation.

There is one object which people are aware of, and think about, more than any other, and this fact is central to understanding human behavior. Human beings are aware of and think about themselves.


## DECISION MAKING

**The Self.** Descartes' famous line was, "I think, therefore I am." He might just as well have said, "I think, therefore I have a Self." Every person has a self. We are all aware of ourselves. We take ourselves into account whenever we act - and this is central to our behavior. You might say that our image of ourselves is the starting point from which we calculate and make decisions as to the best course of action to take in any situation. We are aware of where we are. We are aware, mostly, of our abilities and limitations, our feelings, our wants, our knowledge, and our appearance to others. These are all parts of our self, and we take this awareness into account as we plan and construct our actions and decide what to do in whatever situation we find ourselves (Blumer, 1966).

**Goals.** It is our image of ourselves which ultimately "causes" us to act in one way as opposed to any other. It does so by giving us purpose or *goals*. From our awareness of ourselves, we become aware of our wants and needs. This provides us with a purpose whenever and wherever we are. With this purpose, or goal - couple with our knowledge of the situation around us

- we have a basis for deciding the best course of action to take in that situation. This action/goal association may be simple and immediate, such as scratching yourself to relieve an itch; or the action/goal may be complex and take years to fulfill, such as pursuing a particular career (the action) to earn a comfortable living (the goal). What humans do, they decide to do in order to achieve these goals. Understanding any human's behavior thus involves having some understanding of that person's conception of self, his or her corresponding goals, and their knowledge of the objects/situation around them. This should provide some insight as to what causes that person to decide on one course of action as opposed to any other.

## THE RATIONAL ACT

**Behavior as Separate, Individual Actions.** Underlying this discussion of thinking, decision-making and action is the fact that human behavior does not occur as a seamless flow of activity. People perform separate, individual actions. (Blumer, *Ibid*). Each action consists of the actor manipulating an object, either transporting the object (moving it) or transforming the object (changing it) or both. Actions have a beginning, a middle, and an end. People may or may not be successful as they perform their actions, but it is important to realize and appreciate the separateness of actions. Example: Early this morning, I (among other things) prepared breakfast, ate breakfast, read the newspaper, fed the dog, walked the dog, and prepared lunch. The actions may have overlapped (I ate breakfast and read the newspaper at the same time), but I thought of and performed each one as a separate act.

As a result of this observation, the study of human behavior becomes the study of human *actions*. Asking what causes people to act in certain ways changes to asking what causes people to perform certain actions. For example, if you are interested in studying deviant behavior (say street crime or juvenile delinquency), you would begin by identifying the individual actions that people decided to perform (like mugging a person or skipping school) which are deviant. Then you would investigate why the people involved decided to perform those specific actions. An important point to note, here, is that these actions exist as separate entities in the thinking of the actors *themselves* prior to their performing those actions. As a result, if you or I wish to understand someone else's actions, we need to know how that person conceives of those actions himself or herself.

In noting that humans think and plan ahead before they act as part of the process of achieving their goals, we are saying that they act *rationally*. Humans acquire knowledge of how things "work" in the world by learning from others and through their own experience. We then use that knowledge to predict what will happen if they act in one way or another. People basically think, "If I perform action A, then B will most likely result." This is the essence of a rational act. For example a person may think, "My boss likes hard workers (knowledge). If I work harder and smarter (action), the boss will notice and it might help me get a promotion (the goal)". As Blumer (*Ibid*) noted, however, this rational process can be rather problematic. In performing a particular action in pursuit of a desired goal, the actor may encounter some unforeseen circumstances. The actor may poorly plan his action at the outset. The actor may have failed to take into account some crucial aspect of the situation or something about the situation may unexpectedly change during the course of his action. In the presence of unforeseen circumstances, the actor may have to rethink his plan to reach his goal and thereby alter his actions, or he may decide to abandon his plan altogether.

**The Nine Steps of the Rational Act.** To summarize, thinking, decision-making, and acting are conjoined processes which may be broken down into the following steps: (a) The actor perceives what objects are around him. (b) He identifies and categorizes these objects and considers the relationships between them, including himself. (c) He makes an overall assessment of the situation including his own place within it. (d) He determines his purpose or goal in the situation. (e) He rationally considers what possible actions he might perform (what objects he might act on and how) and what outcomes will likely occur for each of these actions (what will be the final disposition of the objects when he 's done). (f) He determines which action will most likely bring him to his desired goal. (g) He commences to perform the action taking note of how well his "plan" is progressing toward achieving his goal. (h) He adjusts his action or actions, if need be, as the situation changes during the course of his activity. (i) He notes whether or not he was successful in completing his action; and, typically, he will experience satisfaction if he was successful or frustration if he was not. Together, these steps describe the rational act. Many situations are, of course, very familiar to the people in them, and people go through these steps in a very automatic, "unthinking" way. But this process does occur even in the most routine activities.

At this point, we may note that the actions we perform are either directly or indirectly *social* in nature. First of all, the knowledge that people draw on when planning their actions is often acquired from others and from past interaction with others. A person's view of the world and how it works is in large part learned through social interaction. Secondly, and more to the point, people's actions are carried out in concert with other people's actions. When people act, they act with regard to how they think others will *react* to their behavior. Much of a person's thinking and planning involves anticipating how his or her actions will affect others and how other people's actions will affect him or her. This is one way to define social interaction. Social interaction is, at times, simple and easy to understand, such as when one person is buying an item from another at a store. Otherwise, social interaction can be very complex and long lasting, such as in a marriage relationship. Understanding human activity involves understanding, as much as possible, this process by which people act in conjunction with one another.

## Sensitizing Concepts

These facts about thought and action may seem to be little more than common sense and hardly worthwhile to mention. But they have relevance, here, because of the way they direct our inquiry into social interaction. These facts help us to understand social interaction by pointing out what we should be aware of, and some of the questions we should be asking, when we observe what other people are doing and when we try to understand the causes underlying their behavior. To borrow Herbert Blumer's phrase (1954), we might call these "sensitizing" concepts. They help us to be sensitive to *what* actions are being performed and the thought *processes* - the thinking and decision making - that lie behind the actions. Perhaps most importantly, these concepts help us to understand human activity by providing us with specific questions to ask. Trying to analyze and understand human behavior is itself a process, and anyone engaging in this process should be asking many questions. In light of the above discussion of thought and action, these questions would include the following:

What *objects* are the actors aware of and thinking about? What are the meanings of these objects to the actors? How do the actors organize the objects in their situation? What is the actors' overall view of their situation? How do the actors see *themselves* in their situation?

What are the actors' goals? What are the origins or these goals - why do they have them? How do they rationally plan on achieving these goals?

What are the separate actions they are performing - as the actors themselves see and define these actions - in order to achieve their goals?

How are the actors fitting their separate actions together into any ongoing social *interaction*? As the interaction proceeds, are the actors coming closer to reaching their goals? What adjustments are they making to their actions to compensate for changes occurring in the situation?

The answers to the above questions, especially the last few, can be complex and involve a lot of attention to detail. The following chapters discuss much of this detail.

CHAPTER 2

# The Joint Action

● ● ●

EVERY SCIENCE HAS A RELATIVELY few "fundamental" concepts. These are discoveries and ideas which both help define the discipline and serve as a basis for pursuing further research and developing new ideas. In chemistry, these fundamental concepts describe the basic nature of atoms and molecules. In physics, the fundamentals deal with the basic laws governing mass, energy, and motion. In biology, the basics are about the structure and activity of living organisms. In the study of social interaction, the fundamental concepts deal with the self, common understandings, communication, and joint actions.

## HERBERT BLUMER'S JOINT ACTION

Most individual actions, as long as they are social in nature, take place within the context of *joint* actions. Blumer (1966) defines the joint action as "the collective form of action that is constituted by the fitting together of the lines of behavior of the separate participants." A joint action is a *set* of actions performed by two or more individuals. A joint action is thus an *event* which occurs when two or more people act together. Examples of joint actions include contests, such as a basketball game, business meetings, a purchase at a store, a graduation ceremony, and a telephone conversation.

Studying and understanding joint actions is important for a number of reasons. Most importantly, joint actions supply the *frame of reference* that people use when they think, plan ahead, and decide what to do in different situations.

*12*

That is, people conceive of and carry out their separate actions as *parts* of these broader joint actions. As Blumer put it, "the participants fit their acts together, first, by identifying the [joint action] in which they are about to engage and, second, by interpreting and defining each other's acts in forming the joint act. By defining the joint action the participant is able to orient himself; he has a key to interpreting the acts of others and a guide for directing his action with regard to them." (Ibid) For example, swinging at a pitch and trying to get a "hit" is an action which is a logical part of the game of baseball. The game is a joint action involving all the players on both teams, and the batters' actions derive their meaning within the context of the game. By identifying the joint action in which the actors are engaged, each actor has an overall reference for judging the appropriateness of their individual actions.

Since the joint action provides the frame of reference and meaning when people are interacting with one another, it becomes the proper focus of study when trying to understand social interaction. At this point, then, it becomes proper and logical to list and examine some of the common properties of joint actions - their universal characteristics. These universal characteristics include the following:

## Boundaries

Joint actions are separate events. People conceive of them as individual entities (objects). Therefore, joint actions have boundaries. They are bounded by space, time, and participants. A joint action will have a beginning, a middle, and an end. It will take place in certain areas and not in others. And a joint action will involve certain people and not other people. As an event, a joint action may be short, such as a quick purchase at a newsstand, or may be very long and involved, such as a World War.

## Common Understandings.

Joint actions involve common understandings. Common understandings - or shared understandings - are what hold joint actions together.

"Understandings" are the "facts" that people consider - or the knowledge that they use - when they decide what actions to take in a given situation. "Common" understandings are those facts that the participants in a joint action are mutually aware of and agree upon. That is, they have the understandings in common. People rely on a broad range of common understandings as they endeavor to fit their separate actions together into a larger joint action. The common understandings that people use when they interact may be divided into three types:

**Language.** Interaction relies heavily on communication, and communication depends on the actors having a common understanding of the meanings of the sounds they utter, the gestures they make, and the words they write. As such, *language* represents the most essential set of understandings that people hold in common as they interact.

**"Facts".** The second type of common understandings are those that the participants accept as being true and unchanging. These common understandings most often include simple facts about the physical nature of the actors' situation - the objects that make up the actors' environment. For example, for Columbus's voyage in 1492 to make any sense at all, the participants had to agree on the fact that the world was round instead of flat. These "true and unchanging" facts, as a type of common understanding, can include such concerns as religious beliefs, attitudes, and scientific observations. These become "facts" when people who are interacting with one another mutually accept them as being true and unchanging. Accordingly, all information that is assumed to be true and unchanging in a given situation falls into the broader category of common understandings.

**Situational Common Understandings – The Plan.** Situational common understandings are those which are relevant to only the joint action, or situation, at hand. Participants in any joint action use common understandings to anticipate what will happen in successive stages of the joint action. In particular, situational common understandings are vital to being able to predict what other people will do during the course of the joint action. The ability to anticipate what others will do is a key element in all social interaction. Without being able to predict one another's behavior in a situation, people would not be able to fit their actions together to complete any *joint* action. As people engage in a joint action, their interaction can easily fall apart if their understandings of their common situation are not the same.

The situational common understandings which are necessary for any joint action to progress smoothly include:

*What* is the joint action.

What is the joint action's overall *purpose* or *goal*.

*Who* are the logical participants in the joint action and who are not.

*When and where* is the joint action to be performed.

What are the significant *objects* that will be used in the joint action, and

*How* will the joint action be performed. This is a matter of establishing a common understanding of *who* will perform *what actions* in *what sequence* during the joint action. This final common understanding of who does what and when represents the *plan* (Lindesmith, *et al*, p. 174) of action for the joint action's participants. The plan, in turn, supplies the basis for deciding what actions are *logically* appropriate at different points of time during the joint action.

For example, a group of kids playing a baseball game must agree on (a) that they will play baseball and not, say, football; (b) what the goal of the game is (scoring runs, winning); (c) when and where they will play the game; (d) who is on each team and who will play each position; (e) how they will get and use the bats, balls, gloves, bases, etc.; and (f) what the individual ball players will do (what actions they will perform) at different points in the game. All these considerations are the understandings that the different players need to agree on, or hold in common, in order to play the game successfully.

**Consensus.** Finally, not only must the participants in a joint action agree on these different aspects of the joint action, they must also be *aware* that they jointly possess this agreement. Once the actors commonly understand all these different facets of the joint action *and mutually realize* *that they are in agreement*, then the actors are in a position to act on their common understandings and correctly anticipate each other's actions. They must know that they are in agreement for their interaction to progress smoothly. This defines *consensus* (Scheff, 1967). In the example above, the players have to show, through their actions and words, that they do in fact agree on the rules and conditions of the game. Once this final agreement has been reached, then the separate players can confidently proceed being reasonably sure that their actions will "make sense" to one another.

## COMMUNICATION

Since common understandings and consensus are so important to the progress of joint activity, communication is an essential feature of joint actions. People cannot read each other's minds, so they talk, write, and gesture and interpret one another's actions in order to make sure that they each have a common view of their common situation. Communication is typically essential to maintaining consensus when people are interacting. Whenever there is some *lack* of common understandings during a joint action, communication becomes a necessity to get the participants on the same page and to assure that the joint action will progress in a mutually satisfactory way.

**Blumer's Symbolic Interaction: Definition and Interpretation.** When interacting, people communicate *directly* with another by speaking and writing and sharing information about their common situation. People also communicate *indirectly* as they interact by monitoring each other's actions. If one actor notes that another actor is acting as anticipated, the first actor has an assurance that the *joint* action is progressing as expected. If, however, some actor does something unexpected, this can indicate - or communicate - to the others that there is some *mis*understanding about the nature of the situation. Blumer (Ibid) referred to this direct and indirect communication as a process of *definition* and *interpretation* - where we are constantly defining and interpreting each other's understandings and intentions as we observe each other's actions. And, as

*Patterns of Joint Actions*

he noted that our actions have symbolic value in the way they help communicate our intentions to one another, he referred to the whole process as *symbolic interaction*. (This is a phrase that has stuck to the extent that a number of sociologists call themselves Symbolic Interactionists.)

**Fixed vs. Fluid Common Understandings**. The importance of communication varies with the degree to which the common understandings in a joint action are rigid or fluid. Joint actions can be very rigid and predictable, or they can be very fluid and unpredictable. The common understandings in rigidly defined joint actions are set and generally non-negotiable. The common understandings in fluid joint actions may be in question and may need to be constantly discussed and negotiated before and throughout the joint action's progress. If there is enough disagreement between the participants, communication becomes essential to resolving these differences and achieving the consensus necessary to successfully complete the joint action.

**Communication and Relationships.** The communication and common understandings that make joint actions possible also make social relationships possible. When people share, or communicate, their understandings of what they are doing together, they can feel a bonding, or a feeling of being "related" to one another. When they fit together their actions in joint activity, this as well strengthens a feeling of being bonded in a relationship. When people interact repeatedly with one another over time, they tend to strengthen their common understandings and, in turn, their mutual relationships. The next section's discussion of the self will delve into relationships in more detail.

**Similarities vs. Differences with Others.** Underlying this discussion of common understandings, consensus, and communication is the issue of perceived differences versus perceived similarities between people. All people have their differences, and all people have their similarities. The similarities include physical similarities like having - normally - two eyes, a nose, a mouth, two legs, and a brain. People have emotional similarities like having the ability to experience happiness, sadness, satisfaction, and frustration.

And in most situations, people have social similarities such as sharing a common language and being part of a common community. Likewise, all people have their differences. These differences include their names, their overall physical appearance, their tastes in music and food, their backgrounds, and what they like to do in their spare time. The sum total of a person's differences is what makes him or her unique. Important differences that may arise in social situations could include differences in language, different views of "facts" that may be relevant in the situation, and personal goals.

When people encounter one another in a social situation, they often assess one another in terms of how they perceive their similarities and their differences. They become conscious of *how much* alike they are as opposed to how much different they are to one another. If they *think* that they are basically similar to one another, they assume that they see their common situation in a common way. This, then, becomes a basis for obtaining mutual consensus as they interact. That is, to the extent that they see themselves as being alike, they can assume that they have a common perspective, or understanding, of their common situation. With a high degree of consensus, they can typically anticipate one another's actions based on what they themselves would do if they were "in the other person's shoes". As a result, they can proceed to "trust" one another and cooperate smoothly in order to complete the joint action successfully.

If, however, they are conscious of and focus on their differences, they may think that they see their common situation differently and can't anticipate each other's actions. They may even distrust one another's motives. As such, the way actors perceive their similarities versus their differences becomes an important factor in determining how well the actors understand one another and cooperate during the course of a joint action.

We can see the effect of these perceived similarities versus perceived differences in a number of aspects of social life. For one thing, people typically choose their friends based largely on some shared, or similar, interests. As the friends interact focusing on these shared interests, they are likely to be comfortable with one another and interact in a friendly, convivial manner. On the other hand, "prejudice" occurs when people prejudge and act toward others based on the assumption that the others are essentially different from themselves - ignoring their similarities. Most social conflict arises when people focus on their mutual differences and disregard the ways they may be alike. Thirdly, the idea that all people are "created equal", as in our Declaration of Independence, is another way of saying that despite their differences, all people are equally human to the point where they all deserve equal rights and some measure of mutual respect. This attitude, then, has become a guiding principle in the way we govern ourselves as a people.

## THE SELF

**Situational Selves**. Every person has a self. As noted in the previous chapter, we are all aware of ourselves. We take ourselves into account whenever we act - and this is central to our behavior. Our image of ourselves is the starting point from which calculate and decide which actions are best to perform in any situation. We are aware of our physical positions. We are aware, for the most part, of our abilities and limitations, our wants, our knowledge, and our appearance to others. These are all parts of ourselves that we take into account as we plan and construct our actions and decide what to do in whatever joint action we find ourselves. And it is the definitions which we assign to ourselves which ultimately "causes" us to behave in one way as opposed to any other.

Each of us is a *collection* of different selves, each self depending on whatever situation and joint action we find ourselves in. For example, I am a father, an employee, a customer, a voter, and a taxpayer - as well as other identities associated with the different situations I am in during the course of my day. I am a father when I am interacting with my daughter, I am an employee when I am at work, and I am a friend when I am interacting with another friend. In every situation, we have an image of who we are and how we fit in the flow of the ongoing interaction.

Many of the joint actions in which we participate are routine, and in these situations our selves are easily defined. We draw on our memories of previous experiences in similar joint actions, develop expectations of what is likely to happen in the situation, and act accordingly. Being a customer at a store is usually pretty easy since we find ourselves in that situation so often. Being a parent is usually easy and well defined because, after a while, the parent has a lot of experience in parent-child joint actions. But when a person encounters a new situation, he or she is likely to feel some anxiety or self-doubt. A parent whose child has suddenly gotten in trouble (assuming this is a rare occurrence) may wonder what he or she should do in this unusual situation. A new teacher may similarly experience self-doubt the first time she finds herself in a room full of students.

A person's overall view of his or her self is a blend of these different situational, or "elementary", selves (Mead, 1934). The *more* time and personal investment a person spends in a particular type of joint action, the more that corresponding situational self will influence that person's overall view of his or her self. For example, a person's conception of herself as a worker and a mother may be central to her overall identity due to the time and importance she attaches to her career as well as the importance she places on being a mother.

Occasionally, a person can experience personal conflict due to his or her situational selves not "blending" together very well. In the example cited above, the person's self as a worker and her self as a mother can come into conflict if she feels that she isn't devoting enough time to being a mother due to the time she needs to spend at work. As another example, friends typically interact with one another by sharing news and opinions in a mutually respectful, convivial manner. If, however, the friends develop contrasting views on something of importance to them - say, views on religion or politics - the result can present a strain to their relationship. For each person, the individual's self as a friend comes to be at odds with his or her political or religious self. When a person's actions and identity as one elementary self runs contrary to his actions and identity as another self, the result is a phenomenon commonly referred to "role conflict".

**The Looking Glass Self.** To a certain extent, we develop our views of ourselves by observing how others act toward us. This is especially true of children and whenever a person finds himself in a new situation - whenever a situational self is new and untried. By observing how others act act toward us, we conclude how they see us as actors in the situation. Charles Horton Cooley (1902) coined the phrase *"looking glass self"* in describing this phenomenon. It is as if we were looking at ourselves in a mirror when we observe how other people act toward us. We conclude, by watching their actions, how they "see" us, and this affects how we see ourselves. This is how, to a large degree, a person's self develops. Children, especially, find themselves in new and changing joint actions, and they are more dependent on others (especially parents, teachers, etc.) in these situations. As such, their developing ideas of who they are comes largely from how they see other people act toward them.

**Presentation of Self.** Just as we are conscious of ourselves, we are aware of the fact that others develop an image of us as we interact with them. As we interact with others and try to achieve or goals, we make some effort to affect our image of ourselves to others. We try to control how others think of us. This is commonly referred to as *presentation of self* (Goffman, 1959). The basic rationale behind presenting a particular image in a particular situation goes like this: I want to achieve a certain goal. If I am to attain this goal, I need the other person(s) in the joint action to act in a certain way. The other person is more likely to act toward me in the desired way if he identifies, or "sees" *me* in a certain way. I'll present myself in such a manner so that the other person will identify me in that way and act toward me in the desired manner.

We may think of presentation of self as a type of communication that occurs during social interaction. People often do a number of things to present, or communicate, desired images of themselves to others. This includes the way they dress, their "body language", their way of making eye contact, and the way they speak. For example, since it is important to a police officer to get the public to cooperate with him or her, police officers usually present themselves in a particularly stylized way. They dress in a distinctive uniform, they use a formal vocabulary, they usually speak politely and firmly, they use direct eye contact, and they drive distinctive vehicles. All this is to identify themselves in an authoritative manner and to induce others to do what they say.

For another example, someone who wants to show that they are disinterested in what's going on in a situation (for whatever reason) may slouch, yawn, dress more casually than others, and their gaze might wander about while others are speaking. A point to make, here, is that the person may be yawning, slouching, etc. because he or she is genuinely bored with what's going on, or the person might really be interested but may be acting in a disinterested way for some other purpose. It occasionally happens that we ask ourselves if other people are acting the way they truly feel or are they just putting up a false front.

The fact is that our *conscious* or *deliberate* presentation of self is something that exists to a *matter of degree* from situation to situation. This is to say that in many joint actions we act "naturally", with little conscious effort to present a particular image of ourselves to others. But in other joint actions it may be very important to convey a certain impression to others. At those times our presentation of self may be complex, deliberate, and involve much attention to detail. For instance, a person going on a first date may take extraordinary care as to his appearance and how he acts - while that same person would be totally at ease with his appearance and actions when hanging out with an old friend. The degree to which people make a special effort to create an particular image of themselves - and the methods they use to create that image - remains one of the most interesting subjects of social behavior.


## Motivation and Self Realization

What makes a person *want* to do one thing and not something else? When we participate in a joint action, the joint action itself provides us with a *purpose*. The purpose is to do whatever actions are necessary on our part to help compete the joint action successfully. We can call this a *common* purpose as it is a purpose held in common by those engaged in the common joint action. But what makes a person feel good or happy in one situation and feel bad or frustrated in another? What are the sources of people's goals? Understanding the causes that explain social behavior and how we make decisions involves understanding individual motivation.

Whatever people are doing, they want to be successful. A teacher wants to successfully educate his or her students. A mother wants to be successful raising her children. A banker wants to be successful managing money, etc. What all these endeavors describe are efforts of people to "realize" their selves. In any activity, a person has an image, or definition, of his or her self. In these activities, the person will try to make that self real - or successful - through his or her actions. For example, a teacher is a person who educates his pupils - this is what defines someone as a "teacher". The teacher's motivation is to fulfill this definition of his self when he is interacting with his students - educating his students is what makes him a teacher. If the pupils learn the subject matter, then the teacher has successfully done what defines his self in the situation. As a result, the teacher comes to fulfill, or realize, his self. This *self-realization* produces a feeling of accomplishment and satisfaction in the actor. If a person tries and fails to realize his or her self in a situation, he or she will likely feel disappointment or frustration. In a very general sense, self-realization is the *goal* that people strive for when they act in social situations.

Their are two chief ways a self is define in a joint action; and, correspondingly, there are two chief ways a person will try to realize his or her self.

**Task Completion.**First, a person's self may be defined in a joint action by successfully completing a *task*. For example, a salesman in a joint action with a customer is motivated to make a sale. Here, the person's *self* is defined by the task of completing the sale. The person will make decisions and act in a way that will result - hopefully, for the salesman - in a successful completion of this task. When the person does complete the task, he realizes his self and experiences a sense of accomplishment. The following are some more examples of selves that are defined, and realized, by completing tasks:

| Self | Task |
|------|------|
| Carpenter | Building a house or other structure |
| Race car driver | Finishing and (hopefully) winning a race |
| Cook | Preparing a satisfying meal |
| Composer | Writing an enjoyable piece of music |
| Comic | Making people laugh |
| Fisherman | Catching fish |
| Parent | Raising a child to be healthy, happy, and successful |

In each case, the subject will think, decide, and act in ways that the subject calculates will complete the task that defines his or her self. The person will realize his or her self when the task is finished - and then experience self-satisfaction. If the person fails to complete the task, he or she will not realize his or her self and will most likely feel frustration.

**Relationship Fulfillment.** A person participating in a joint action can also have his or her self defined by his or her *relationship* with others involved in the joint action. Here, the *self* exists as a *part* of a larger whole. The larger whole is the relationship. For example, a person cannot be a husband without a wife. He cannot be a boss without a subordinate, a salesman without a buyer, or a friend without another friend. One does not exist without the other. The self is defined through the relationship.

In this case, the person tries to realize his or her self by completing the conditions which define the relationship in the joint action. As discussed above, any relationship exists by virtue of the common understandings which exist between the participants. These common understandings enable the actors to anticipate one another's actions and to cooperate with one another. The acting individual, here, is motivated to cooperate and act in accordance these common understandings which define the relationship. When the participants in the joint action act together successfully,

*Patterns of Joint Actions*

they in effect make their relationship real, and in turn they realize their respective selves. On the other hand, if the participants in a joint action come to have differing understandings of their common situation, their interaction breaks down and, likewise, their relationship breaks down. As a result, their "selves" - as defined by the relationship - become unfulfilled.

Since this is a more complicated process, I'll list its components:

a) Common understandings and cooperation between actors are necessary to make a joint action work.

b) These common understandings and the cooperation define a relationship between the actors.

c) The actors in the joint action see themselves as parts of this relationship.

d) The actors are then motivated to act in accord with these common understandings that define the relationship and make the joint action work.

e) When the participants cooperate successfully in the joint action, they are able to perceive their relationship working. Their relationship is realized when they are able to successfully complete the joint action.

f) Since the individual defines his or her self by the relationship, the participant realizes his or her self as the relationship is realized. When these conditions occur, the actors typically experience a feeling of self-satisfaction.

Team sports provide a good example of self-realization through fulfilling relationships. Any team effort requires the close cooperation of the separate team members. Aside from the outcome of any contest they may engage in, the team members' cooperation, or "team work", creates bonds between the participating individuals. The actors' joint activity makes the team a reality and gives each actor an identity as a part of the team. Being able to cooperate with one another successfully (making a good "team effort") strengthens these bonds with one another and strengthens each individual team member's identity as a teammate. People typically experience a pleasurable feeling from their participation in a team effort because their activity reaffirms their relationships with their teammates and, consequently, their identity as team members. This feeling of self-satisfaction can even exist to some degree when the team loses a game. Even in the face of a loss, the team's joint action still serves the purpose of fulfilling the players' identities, or selves, as members of the team.

In most joint actions, people define their selves *both* in terms of completing a task *and* in terms of their relationships with other participants in the joint action. That is, task completion and relationship fulfillment often go hand in hand. When one happens, so does the other. In a typical, smooth running joint action, the actors consider their common situation, they rely on common understandings to anticipate one another's actions, and cooperate with one another by completing their respective tasks. As they do so, they are defining and realizing their respective selves by simultaneously completing their tasks and realizing their relationships with one another. Consider a parent helping her son with a homework assignment. The parent has the task of helping her son complete the assignment and is motivated to complete this task successfully. By so doing, she is also fulfilling and strengthening her relationship with her son - their relationship is built on the common understanding that the parent will help her child when help is needed. The parent realizes her self (being a good parent) by both completing a task (getting the assignment done) and fulfilling the relationship (helping the child).

Joint actions often differ, however, by the *degree* to which self-realization is based on completing a task versus fulfilling a relationship. In some joint actions, task completion may take precedence over relationship fulfillment; and in other joint actions relationship fulfillment is the primary concern. For example, in a competitive joint action, which pits one individual against another, such as in a chess match or a track meet or a trial, self-realization is chiefly based on task completion, like winning a prize or a game or a legal decision. In these joint actions, relationships are not the primary focus. People in these joint actions will do whatever they think is necessary to complete their task with little regard to how their actions affect others. When people try to realize their selves through task completion alone, they may try to deceive the other people in the joint action or they may even hate them. The familiar phrases, "all's fair in love, war, and politics" and "the end justifies the means" apply in situations where task completion has primary importance over relationship fulfillment.

In other joint actions, the emphasis may be on relationship fulfillment. Ceremonies, celebrations, and parties are examples of activities that focus on the relationships between the participants more than the completion of some task. These joint activities have the chief purpose of affirming the common understandings and the mutual relationships between the participants. The success or failure of the joint action is often judged by how well the actors' mutual bonds are strengthened as the joint action progresses. Many of these joint actions are very ritualized, and the behavior of the actors is highly stylized having the primary purpose of demonstrating and reinforcing the actors' relationships. Marriage ceremonies, religious services, formal dinners, holiday celebrations, and even "dates" are examples of activities in which the participants' actions are often highly ritualized and are focused on defining and strengthening the relationships between the actors.

To sum up, this chapter has focused on the the *joint action* as the fundamental unit of social interaction. When people interact, they have an overall purpose in mind and, for the most part, a common goal to achieve, and they perform an action together, or jointly, in order to achieve it. They execute a *plan* of mutual action, fitting their actions together in a way which they reason will produce the desired result. This overall purpose and the plan that they employ comprise a set of *understandings* which the actors necessarily hold in *common* in order to effectively coordinate their actions. As people interact, they take into account one another's actions and note whether or not the joint action is progressing according to their conception of the overall plan. As they deem necessary, the actors *communicate* with one another about what they are doing, and the disposition of the objects acted on, in order to facilitate the joint action's progress. While interacting, the actors' ability to recognize their mutual similarities (how alike they are to one another), as opposed to their differences, provides a useful tool to help anticipate each other's actions as the joint action develops and circumstances change.

In each joint action, each actor has a *self* which he defines in terms of some *task* (or tasks) he is to perform and in terms of the relationships he has with the other actors in the situation. If the joint action is performed successfully, the actors will have performed their respective tasks and fulfilled the requirements of their mutual relationships; and as a result, the actors will realize their respective selves in the joint action. This *self-realization* gives the actors a feeling of self-satisfaction and self-fulfillment and provides the basis for the actors' motivation while performing the joint action. Conversely, if a joint action falls apart for some reason, the actors will fail to realize their selves and consequently experience frustration at the turn of events. In all of this, the joint action provides the frame of reference and overall context within which individual actions get their purpose and meaning.

# CHAPTER 3

# Patterns of Joint Actions

● ● ●

WHEN PEOPLE ENGAGE IN JOINT actions, those joint actions rarely "stand alone" as isolated, singular events. People engage in *patterns* of joint actions. The purpose of this chapter is to discuss four different ways people form these patterns of joint actions. The first two patterns discussed - routines and careers - focus on individual actors and their motivations. The second two types of patterns - group activity and networks - focus on the joint activity which occurs within and between social groups.

## ROUTINES

A routine is a series of joint actions which are, to the people who engage in them, very similar and which occur repeatedly. Purchasing items in a grocery store, for example, is something that we do repeatedly, routinely. The joint actions that we engage in at work or school are typically very similar from one day to the next and, therefore, part of a routine. Other examples of routines are family meals, going to religious services, and weekly shopping trips.

In joint actions which are part of a routine, the common understandings involved are usually well established. Since the activity has been repeated before, the actors are generally familiar with (a) the setting, (b) the objects involved, (c) the respective self-definitions of the actors, and (d) the plan - who will do what and when. Cooperation, therefore, is typically smooth in a routine joint action, and the actors usually need to negotiate or iron out details with one another only to a minimal degree during the joint action's course.

It is important to keep in mind that joint actions vary to the *degree* in which they are routine to the actors involved. Some joint actions are very similar to past joint actions and others are less so. In general, the more routine the joint actions are, the more established the common understandings and relationships between the actors will be. The less routine the joint actions are, the more the actors will need to communicate and negotiate with one another in order to complete the joint action. In addition, in some situations the joint action may be routine to one actor but may be a new experience for some other actor. In this case, the more "experienced" actor will likely have to explain and establish the common understandings of the joint action to the less experienced actor. The more experienced person will consequently often be able to dictate the plan that the actors will follow during the joint activity.

In routine joint actions, the major emphasis is on acting in accord with the common understandings that exist between the actors. The actors expect one another to act in a certain way, and any deviation from the expected pattern of interaction can, if not adequately "explained" by the deviating actor, cause a significant problem. If someone deviates from the established common understandings, not only will the current joint action be disrupted, but it may affect future joint actions which are part of this routine. That is, if a person violates some common understandings in one situation, those understandings may come into question in future similar situations. This would, in turn, raise doubts about the ability of the actors to reliably anticipate one another's actions and call into doubt the nature of an otherwise established routine.

This emphasis on acting in accord with established common understandings in routines places a strong emphasis on self-realization through relationship fulfillment in these situations. Just as the common understandings used in routine joint actions are well established, the relationships between the participants are likewise well established, and fulfilling these relationships comes to have primary importance for the actors

*Patterns of Joint Actions*

involved. To put this in other terms, much of the way we think of ourselves comes from the relationships we have with other people, and these relationships are forged and strengthened in routine, day to day joint actions. Even though these routine joint actions usually involve completing some task or other, the identity of the individuals and the order of their lives becomes so entrenched in these relationships that the tasks involved, while still being important, can become subordinate in importance to maintaining the established relationships in the routine.

To illustrate this point, imagine being at a store and trying to buy a particular item which is clearly marked as to its price, but the cashier insists on charging you ten cents more for the item. The ten cents may be an insignificant amount of money, but charging you more for the item than the marked price violates a fundamental common understanding in what would otherwise be a routine transaction. The cashier's action calls into question the relationship between the two of you and even, perhaps, calls into question just *who you are* in the situation. The cashier's action may ultimately threaten your sense of self and likely cause an intense feeling of frustration. The struggle for civil rights in the 1960's often involved situations, such as sit-ins at lunch counters, in which black people were denied equal treatment in joint actions which were otherwise routine for white people.

## CAREERS

As well as routines, people participate in joint actions which, together, constitute a *career*. A person is engaged in a career when he or she participates in a number of joint actions in an effort to reach some long range goal. In this case, the actor participates in the joint actions as *unique* and *necessary* parts of a longer sequence of activity. That is, the successful completion of one joint acton is often essential to the completion of some *greater*, or higher order, action. When this happens, engaging in the smaller, immediate joint action exists as an *integral part* of the actor's larger career. For example, making a sale - a smaller joint action - is typically part of the larger action of running a business. Also, a cross examination is a joint action which is an integral part of a court trial.

When a person participates in a joint action which is part of a career, the participant's motivation focuses on the completion of some task. If the task is not completed successfully, the outcome of the career may become jeopardized - the actor may not achieve his or her long term goal. As such, the actor's self-definition and self-realization are likewise oriented toward the completion of this task. Consider the examples in the above paragraph. If a business owner fails to complete some important deal (the task), his or her business may suffer - possibly even to the point of going out of business. Likewise, an effective cross examination in a trial may be crucial to achieving the desired outcome of the trial. In both examples, the actor's participation in the immediate joint action is part of an ongoing career; and in each case, the actor wants to complete some immediate task. The successful completion of this task will then have a positive effect on the progress of his or her career. The actor's self is defined with respect to completing the given task, and his or her self-realization will depend on whether or not he or she accomplishes that task successfully.

When a person participates in a joint action, it is often *both* part of a routine and part of a career. A "class" at a school or university is a good example. Classes occur, as a rule, on a routine basis. The settings are similar, and the common understandings and relationships between the students and the instructors are stable and predictable. Classes also occur as parts of the academic careers of the students and instructors involved. A class is part of a course - it is a joint action which is an essential part of the overall course. The course, in turn, is a larger joint action which students participate in as part of their overall academic careers. By the time people become adults, most of the joint actions in which they participate have a routine character to them *and* are part of a career of activity. Work joint actions especially are typically both routine and part of a career of interrelated joint actions.

The above discussions of routines and careers necessarily focus on the situations of the *individual actors* engaged in the joint actions in question.

*Patterns of Joint Actions*

That is, if a joint action is part of a routine, it is so because of the past experience of the separate actors involved. In some situations, the same joint action may be a routine event for one participant but not routine for another. Similarly, if the actors in a joint action are engaged in careers, they are engaged in separate careers - each actor has his or her own career, and each has their own long term goals to pursue. In these cases, joint actions are meaningfully connected in separate and possibly different ways for the separate actors. Likewise, the *consequences* of any joint action's outcome - its effects on the participants - will often differ for each of the actors involved.

## SOCIAL GROUPS

The next step is to examine how joint actions can affect one another, and form a pattern, in the context of social groups.

For the purposes of this chapter, a "social group" will refer to a number of people who interact with one another and who think of themselves as members of the same group. Examples of small groups would be families, scout troops, and small businesses. Mid-sized groups would include organizations such as union locals, churches, companies with over 100 employees, and most high schools. Large groups would include institutions such as the army, multi-national corporations, state governmental bodies, and universities. Membership in social groups and organizations is so pervasive a part of our social existence that some sociologists treat these groups as their chief focus of analysis. (As a note, sociologists also refer to "social groups" in the manner of groups of people who do not necessarily interact with one another but who share some socially relevant characteristic, such as having a particular religious affiliation, ethnic type, or sexual orientation. The relevance of the distinction between these two "types" of groups will be discussed in depth in Chapter 8.)

People form groups (the first type) and participate in them in order to achieve some primary goal or other. That is, groups have some purpose for being which the members of the group recognize and (generally) subscribe to. The primary purpose of a business is to make money, the primary purpose of a city government is to provide necessary services to the community, the primary purpose of a school is to educate, etc. In addition, there are commonly one or more "secondary" purposes for a group's existence. Simply socializing and getting to know other people is a secondary purpose in many groups such as sports teams and charitable organizations. But the reason people will form a group in the first place will be in order to achieve some specific goal, and this defines the group's primary purpose.

The activity of a social group is essentially a greater, or extended joint action. The members of the group engage in this joint action in order to achieve the group's goal. Running a business, having church services, attending school are the joint actions within which the individual members perform their separate actions in order to accomplish the group's purpose. Being a *greater* joint action, this joint action is typically comprised of many (perhaps millions, in the case of governments and corporations) of shorter joint actions. Each shorter joint action is performed as an integral part of fulfilling and completing the greater joint action. Running an assembly line, therefore, is a smaller but necessary part of running General Motors; just as "registration" is a relatively short joint action, but a necessary part of the university experience.

We can say, then, that the activity of social groups typically consists of a *set* of smaller joint actions. The set of smaller joint actions forms a pattern by virtue of the fact that the smaller joint actions are *functionally related* to one another. Each shorter joint action is performed to accomplish some *task* which is deemed necessary for the completion of the group's larger, overall joint action. We can use the example of General Motors, again, to illustrate this point:

The overall goal of General Motors is to make a profit by making and selling vehicles. In order to do this, GM engages in numerous separate joint actions, each joint action performing some function necessary to achieving this goal. Maintenance workers care for the facilities. Assembly line workers put together the vehicles. Accountants manage the books and make expenditures. Dealers sell the cars and trucks. And executives have meetings to coordinate these many joint actions so that the corporation realizes a profit. These are all separate joint actions, but they each perform some task which is necessary to accomplish the corporation's goal. They form a pattern in the way they are functionally related to one another within the context of the corporation's greater joint action.

## LINKS AND NETWORKS

In addition to the way joint actions can be interrelated within a social group, joint actions often occur between members of *different* groups. These joint actions form a *link* between these groups with the result being a social *network*. Often, these links allow for the flow of objects and information from one group to the other to each group's mutual benefit. For example, whenever General Motors employees buy parts from another company, the buyers and sellers engage in a joint action, and that joint action links the two organizations together, with each company benefiting from the transaction. This link will become especially strong and will form a relationship between the two groups if the joint action occurs repeatedly and routinely. If the link between the two groups is strong enough, the joint action forming the link will often have critical importance for the fortunes for one or more of the two groups. Going back to the above example, if GM stops buying parts from a particular supplier, that supplier may may lose enough business to eventually send it into bankruptcy. In the present state of economic globalization, the links between banks, governments, and multinational corporations are so strong and intertwined that failure of one institution in one country (say, in Greece or China) can adversely affect businesses half way around the world.

In addition to the patterns of joint actions which typically exist within and between groups, there are a few characteristics of social interaction in groups that are worth mentioning at this point:

As discussed above, a fundamental characteristic of social groups is that they are comprised of a pattern of functionally related joint actions. We may also note that many of these joint actions are repetitive in nature. That is, the same or similar joint actions will be performed regularly - either every day, every week, or every month - by members of the group. For example, most businesses and governmental bodies have a standard workday, and schools have regularly scheduled school days and school years. These repeated joint actions thus form regularly scheduled *routines* in the life of the social group. Once these routines are established, they form the basis for the group members' relationships with one another, and they often have a very significant effect on the members' self-definitions and motivations.

The successful completion of any joint action requires the existence of common understandings between the participants. As outlined earlier, the common understandings are necessary to ensure the proper cooperation of the actors and ensure that the participants reach their goals. In larger groups, some of these understandings often evolve into strict codes of rules and procedures to follow. As the size of a group increases and becomes more complex, there is a greater need to formalize common understandings to make sure that the interaction of the group goes smoothly. Manuals, codes of conduct, mission statements, laws, conferences, forms, seminars, and compliance departments are often assumed to be necessary to keep the joint activity of the group sufficiently coordinated and avoid mishaps.

When a *link* exists and persists between two organizations, the process can have particularly interesting consequences. As discussed in chapter two, when individuals interact with one another over a significant period of time, they can develop an increasingly strong relationship with one another. Their common understandings and their ability to anticipate one another's actions increases, and they can become "like minded". The actors often come to understand one another to the extent that each actor can easily imagine being in the other's position - how and why they make their respective decisions.

## The Circulation of Elites and The Military Industrial Complex

In the case of joint activity linking two separate groups, the actors can additionally come to understand how and why the mutually separate groups operate. The actors can become more and more intimate with the workings of each other's group, and occasionally one actor will *literally* take a role in the other group. This process of changing roles between interacting groups commonly acts to strengthen the relationship between the groups. As a frequent example of this process, government officials who deal with large corporations and banks often retire from their government positions, when their pensions are secured, to take jobs with the corporations and banks they have been dealing with. For instance, between 1997 and 2003, fifty-three United States government officials left their positions to take jobs at Boeing Corp., a large government contractor. The sociologist C. Wright Mills noted this phenomenon in describing "the circulation of elites" (Mills,1956); and Dwight D. Eisenhower alluded to this procedure when he warned against the influence of the "military-industrial complex" in 1960. In each case, the warning is that the interests of one group become the interests of people in another group to the possible detriment of people outside the groups, such as taxpayers and the general public.

## Social Conflict

The fact that people engage in joint actions which both (a) play an important part in their individual careers and routines *and* (b) are part of a group's greater joint activity - with its own overall plan and purpose - presents a frequent source of social conflict. The need for the group to achieve its overall purpose may not adequately accommodate the needs of the individual members of that group. Individuals may feel exploited or otherwise dissatisfied if their participation in the group is not personally rewarding. The classic example of this conflict lies in corporate labor - management relations. Here, conflict may arise as workers endeavor to maximize their pay and benefits while managers try to increase the group's profits by limiting these costs. As one possible solution, managers of large organizations frequently look for new and creative ways to measure and increase their members' feeling of "engagement" and self-worth in their organizations. They do this in an effort to decrease this conflict without significantly increasing their costs.

To sum up, this chapter defines and discusses four different patterns of joint actions: routines, careers, group joint actions, and networks of joint actions. Routines and careers are patterns that individuals engage in in their day to day activities. Routines are composed of joint actions which are similar and which people engage in on a more or less regular basis. When involved in a routine joint action, the actor's self-definition and self-realization are oriented toward relationship fulfillment. Careers are patterns of extended activity which people engage in with long term goals in mind. When engaged in careers, individuals participate in joint actions in order to complete steps that they deem to be necessary to proceed to their ultimate goals. In these joint actions, the individual's self-definition and self-realization are oriented toward the successful completion of one or more tasks.

In addition, human beings belong to social groups and participate in the activity of those groups. We may define a group's activity as a larger (relatively speaking) joint action which people engage in to accomplish the group's overall purpose. This larger group joint action is typically comprised of a set of smaller, interrelated joint actions. These smaller joint actions are interrelated in the sense that they each complete some task and fulfill some *function* which is deemed necessary for the group to achieve its overall goal.

In the fourth case, people in one group often interact with people in other groups in efforts to further their respective group's aims. The joint

*Patterns of Joint Actions*

actions that people engage in *between* groups *link* those groups together into wider *networks* of joint activity. Especially in the realm of economic interaction, these networks of joint activity will often reach across borders and, if certain joint actions fail, that failure can have extremely far reaching and damaging consequences.

Finally, it has been worthwhile to note that the patterns of individuals' joint actions (routines and careers) are typically incorporated into patterns of group activity. People become members of social groups in order to realize their own separate goals and their own separate selves. The group's identity and purpose are often somewhat different. In the ideal case, the goals of the group's separate members and the overall goals of the group complement one another. The success of the group and the ability of the individual members' to realize their selves coincide. But this is not always the case.

CHAPTER 4

# Five Factors

● ● ●

THE SELF, COMMON UNDERSTANDINGS, COMMUNICATION, and the joint action have been presented here as the essential components of social interaction. Each plays a part in *all* social interaction. But the character of social interaction can also be richly varied and often complex. There are many factors which *may or may not* play a part in different joint actions. A change in the physical environment, for instance, may have an effect on some joint actions but not others. *Cause and effect* relationships in social interaction, as a separate topic, will be treated in a later chapter of this book. At this point, however, it may be helpful to discuss five factors which may or may not influence social interaction, based on circumstances, by having an effect on motivation.

## PHYSIOLOGICAL AND PSYCHOLOGICAL NEEDS

The most obvious class of factors which affect joint actions are our physiological needs. We all have the need for food, clothing, and shelter. In short, in our modern world, we need money. This need typically motivates us to obtain jobs or some other sort of business career. That is, virtually all of us find ourselves involved in daily routines (jobs) and long term careers in our efforts to obtain money. Secondly, humans also have psychological needs for companionship and intimacy. These needs compel people to establish relationships of friendship and love which, in turn, compels people to engage in certain patterns of joint actions. Courtship, for example, is

*40*

a career in which people engage in order to find a lover. Courtship can also involve various routines such as dating and regular telephone conversations. Thirdly, children have similar needs and, being dependent on adults, they have a need for care and nurturing. To satisfy these needs, people establish the set of relationships which constitute a family, and the parents engage in the routines and career of "raising" a family.

In each case, our physiological and psychological needs typically give us various goals which we endeavor to obtain. As a result, these needs motivate us to engage in various routines and careers in order to achieve these corresponding goals. As a general factor which affects joint actions, then, physiological and psychological needs play a large part in motivating people to *purposefully begin* participating in particular careers and routines and to follow through in these careers and routines in order to satisfy these needs.

## VALUES

Webster's dictionary defines a value as a "desirable or esteemed characteristic, principle, or quality". Many things can be valued, such as a particular vintage of wine, a style of architecture, or Chevrolets as opposed to Fords. As consumers, we are motivated to possess objects which have particular characteristics as opposed to objects which do not.

Sociologists (as well as many politicians, clergy, and journalists) primarily use the term "values" with regard to characteristics of people and their behavior. Values are personal traits and qualities which people in a community commonly understand to be desirable or important to possess. A few examples of values are patriotism, individualism, entrepreneurship, honesty, religious faith, helping others, loyalty to friends and family, hard work, and sacrifice. These are personal characteristics which are commonly perceived in our society as being desirable. These values reveal themselves (or fail to reveal themselves if people are "lacking" in values) in the way people interact with one another in different situations. Values are frequently equated with morality, and strongly held values are frequently deemed to be an essential part of a healthy community. The significance of values is such that sociologists, politicians, journalists, and civic leaders often see the *lack* of values as a primary cause of social conflict and disorder. The following are a few more detailed observations about values.

Values, as personal traits, help to facilitate the successful completion of joint actions. Or, to put it another way, certain personal traits are judged to be helpful (and in many cases essential) to the successful completion of various joint actions, and these traits are often collectively referred to as values. As mentioned earlier, an essential feature of joint actions is that the people involved understand one another and are able to anticipate one another's behavior. That is, as long as people trust one another to act *in a certain way* in different situations, their joint activity will generally be cooperative and - barring unforeseen circumstances - come to a successful conclusion. As people interact with one another in a variety of situations, they come to recognize certain personality traits which help build this trust and facilitate their interaction. For example, being honest or "keeping your word" are personal traits (values) which enable people to trust one another and cooperate smoothly as they interact. Being a hard worker is a trait which people see as important as they interact with one another on the job. Being religious is seen by many people as a sign that the individual can be trusted to act in line with the dictates of whatever religion they share. As a result, people come to "value" these general characteristics of behavior which they see as necessary, or at least helpful, to the successful completion of their joint activity. Values, thus, tend to *evolve* out of interaction as the actors recognize what traits make people more reliable and dependable in their joint activity. And, since the valued trait or behavior can play a part in a variety of situations, the "traits" involved are typically broadly defined.

Values, being personality traits and characteristics, help to describe and define the Self. People either possess a valued trait and display it as they interact with others, or they do not; and this helps shape how people define and "know" and identify one another. For example, a parent may be described as a Good Christian parent if that person displays the traits which other people associate with being a good Christian. A social service volunteer who is especially caring and helpful could be seen as such by other members of the community, and this may help shape their perception of the volunteer. In these instances, the values are characteristics which people in the community commonly regard as important to have, and when a person displays that value, other people in the same community are apt to respond by thinking more highly of that person. Possessing esteemed values is typically seen as a sign of "character" in the actor. As people often feel better about themselves when others appreciate their behavior and "character", values can consequently motivate people and play a part in self-realization. This process may be summarized in the following sequence:

(a) A person will think of (or define) his or her self with regard to some particularly valued trait, such as being smart or being patriotic.
(b) The person "acts out" or displays this valued trait as he or she interacts with others.
(c) Other people recognize that the person has this trait.
(d) The others show their approval of the person for having this trait.

The "approval" shown may come in the form of personal praise or simply showing appreciation for the subject's efforts in some joint activity. As a result of this show of approval, the person comes to realize his/her self and experience some degree of self-satisfaction. A child being congratulated by her parents for doing well on a test is a simple example of this process. The valued traits are intelligence and hard work. The child displays these traits by doing well on the test. The parents recognize the traits and show their approval by congratulating the child. The child realizes her self - as she defines herself as being smart and a hard worker - and experiences self-satisfaction by experiencing her parents' approval.

Values may or may not have a great effect on people's actions as they interact with one another in different situations. Values play a more significant part during social interaction when the relationships between the actors have become well established and when the joint actions in which they are engaged are part of stable routines. When a person "acts out" some value or other, other people who witness the actions are apt to respond approvingly. That is, a person's image in the eyes of others typically improves when that person is able to show his or her "strength of character" in different situations. This approval is most apt to be important to an actor when the actor strongly cares what the others think of him or her. When the relationships and routines that an actor has with others are strong and play a large part in the actor's overall definition of his or her self, values become more significant and have a greater effect on his or her actions. Conversely, when a person's routines and relationships are more fractured and fleeting, values will play a lesser part in the person's decisions and actions.

Along these same lines, we may note that values have a greater effect during social interaction in "closely knit" communities. A closely knit community is one in which the same people interact with one another in a variety of joint actions. It is a community in which people's careers and routines often intersect and are tied, or knit, together. In such a community, the same people will be more likely to interact with one another at church and at a store as well as at work and at the local school. In such a community, people come to know one another and depend on one another in a number of ways and in a number of settings. Consequently, here, a person's reputation or character plays an important part in his/her joint activity with others. If a person's values are strong, others will judge that person to be dependable and worth interacting with in future situations. Conversely, if a person becomes "unreliable" in one joint action, it will have a negative effect on how others judge that person's character and how they will interact with that person in other joint actions in other situations. In a community that is *not* closely knit, what a person does or says will have less impact on his or her future activity because the other people that the person is interacting with will be less likely to play a part in the person's other joint activity.

Taking this train of thought one step further, we can see why some people decry the "decline" in values in modern society. People in modern society, as opposed to past, more "traditional" societies, are more mobile and employ more "mass" communication. As people move around more and communicate with more strangers over longer distances, there is a decline in the frequency with which the same people interact with one another in a variety of situations. That is, people are more frequently interacting with others that they will never see or talk to again. This decreases the accountability that people have with one another. If a person is less than honest with another person, that dishonesty will have a lesser impact on the dishonest person if those two people will never interact with one another again. Some people consequently see urbanization and the faster, more fluid nature of modern life in a suspicious way because they see these developments as a threat to accountability and a decline in moral values.

In addition, some people may judge that values are in a state of decline in modern society as a result of the fact that modern societies are often more diverse and fragmented than older, more traditional societies. A value that one segment of society may adopt may be rejected by other segments of society. For example, styles of hair and dress often vary with some styles being looked at with distain by many while being adopted with approval by others. As another example, many may see a disruptive or rebellious attitude as being a valued trait which is necessary if people are to enact what they perceive to be needed social change. The same trait will likely feared by others who are content with the status quo.

Since values are personal characteristics which help make joint actions proceed more smoothly and successfully, sociologists have often regarded values as the "glue" which holds society together. Many sociologists envision society as a "structure" composed of many parts. These parts need something to bind them to one another and hold the larger structure together. These sociologists see values as the stuff which serves this purpose. They see people rewarding good behavior and punishing bad behavior as the behavior either conforms to accepted values or not. In doing so, sociologists see people acting to *reinforce* the adoption of important values in one another. As people act in conformity to accepted values, their interaction with one another proceeds more smoothly, and the society as a whole prospers. Accordingly, these sociologists consider strongly held values - and people acting in ways to reinforce these values - as being critical to a stable, efficiently running society.

A problem with this way of looking at values is that it does not quite properly describe the role that values play in social interaction. The most important issue as people interact is whether or not the joint actions they engage in proceed to a successful conclusion. The personal, "valued" characteristics that people display as they interact often facilitate their interaction, but they may not be crucial to the interaction's successful conclusion. Negotiation, persuasion, tangible rewards, and threats of punishment may be equally effective in assuring mutual cooperation during the course of joint activity. The important point, here, is to recognize *the way* in which values play a part in joint actions and *the degree* to which values affect the course of certain joint actions as opposed to others.

One final note about values has to do with the significance of language. In chapter two, we discussed two ways people define their selves: by completing tasks and by fulfilling relationships. When a person completes a task, he or she is *performing an action* - he or she is *doing* something - and a *verb* is most closely associated with the person's self definition. When a person fulfills a relationship, that person becomes a *part* of something larger (the relationship), and *nouns* are primarily associated with his or her self definition. Nouns and verbs are the parts of speech most clearly used when defining the self in these two ways.

When a person possesses some valued trait, however, he or she has some *modifier* (an adjective or adverb) attached to his or her self definition. A *religious* person or a *brave* soldier or a *dedicated* employee possesses a trait that is valued, and that valued trait is noted by virtue of the adjectives used. When that person experiences approval from others for having that trait, he or she typically experiences a feeling of self-satisfaction. He or she realizes his/her self as that self is defined by that modifier. Thus, with valued traits being added to a person's self definition, the person's overall self becomes more whole - we might say more grammatically complete. The self becomes defined via adjectives and adverbs as well as by nouns and verbs.

## Status and Conspicuous Consumption

At this point, we've described how people define their selves in terms of completing tasks, by being part of relationships, and by possessing (or not possessing) certain valued traits. Closely related to these ways that people think of themselves has to do with making comparisons. When people think of themselves, they very often make comparisons between themselves and others.

People want to be successful; or to put it another way, people want to make a success of themselves. A common way people measure this success is by comparing themselves to others. For an obvious example, a student who gets B's is a good and successful student. But a student who gets A's is normally considered to be a better student. If a salesperson who generates $100,000 in sales is deemed to be successful, then a salesperson who generates $200,000 will be deemed to be a more successful and better salesperson. In these cases, the actor not only realizes her self by achieving a certain level of accomplishment, she may *further* realize her self (and experience greater self satisfaction) by being "better" than others who are doing the same thing. **Status** refers to the "position" that a person has relative to others when comparisons such as these are made. The better, or higher, a person compares to another, the higher is that person's status.

There are many ways people make comparisons with one another, and consequently, status can take on many forms. Money is probably the most commonly used basis for making comparisons between people. People with more money are often (though not always) considered to be more successful than others and, as such, frequently have higher status than people with less money in their community. Other than money, a number of different criteria may be used to measure success and status in different situations. *Grades* are used as a basis for comparing students. *Power* - the ability to dictate to others who will do what in a joint action - can be used as a basis for measuring success and status within a social group. When a person possesses some special *skill* or *talent* in performing some self-defining task, such as cooking or carpentry or some athletic skill, then that person may be compared to others with regard to that skill and may receive some heightened degree of status as a result.

How well a person displays a community's values can also affect that person's standing, or status, in his or her community. The better a person acts in conformity with his or her community's values, the more tacit approval that person will likely receive from others with regard to his/her behavior. A person's "reputation" is often a measure of how well he or she conforms to these values. The measure of approval received can then become a basis for comparison which people may use to help establish that person's status in the community. In this case, even a person of modest means can achieve an elevated measure of status by virtue of the way he or she adheres to the accepted values that the community holds.

This tendency to compare oneself to others and to realize one's self by trying to be better than others manifests itself in interesting ways. In general, it is possible to list five basic ways that the pursuit of higher status can affect people's day to day routines and careers:

Status can affect a person's decisions as to what professions to engage in. Studies have shown that people in a community largely agree as to how prestigious different professions are relative to one another. That is, people typically agree on how to *rank* professions, and so they agree on which professions are better than others. As a result, a person who wants to establish a higher degree of status for himself or herself may choose to pursue a prestigious career, such as a doctor, or lawyer, or college professor or professional athlete. Factors such as a person's abilities, time, and resources will of course also affect that person's decisions in choosing a career, but the pursuit of status is often a primary concern in this decision making process.

Similarly, status considerations can motivate a person to work harder in his or her chosen career. Whenever a person can be compared to others, there is the potential motivation to improve his or her status by working harder and achieving more. Athletes, businessmen, community volunteers, politicians, and even parents are often motivated to strive a bit more and to accomplish more relative to other athletes, businessmen, etc., in their community for the sake of achieving higher status.

People often create and perpetuate particular ways of comparing themselves with others in order to create higher status for themselves at the expense of others. It is often the case that people in a community will see some set of others as being "different" from themselves and use that difference as a basis for comparison - saying that the others who are different are bad or inferior compared to themselves. This process usually works only if the "different" people are in a minority in the community or are without much economic or political power.

Racism, as an example, is consequently a byproduct of people making comparisons between themselves and others. Racism, as well as other forms of discrimination, is often most virulent among lower and working class people - that is, among people who don't have much wealth and status in their community. As these people perceive their own status as relatively low, they may discriminate against racial and cultural minorities for the sake of maintaining their own place "above" them. Thus, working class or lower middle class people have on occasion responded violently to the arrival of racial minorities in their neighborhoods whereas upper or upper middle class people have been less likely to do so. The violent response is a result of their fear of losing some degree of what little status they have.

In the more common case, discrimination works as people in the majority find ways to exclude members of a minority from joint actions in which they are themselves engaged. By refusing to interact with members of the minority, the members of the majority often effectively thwart careers and routines that members of the minority want to engage in; and, in consequence, they thwart efforts of the minority to improve their status in the community. By impeding the minority's efforts to improve their status, the discrimination will reinforce any stereotype that the minority members are "naturally" inferior to members of the majority.

*Conspicuous consumption* (Veblen, 1899) is a byproduct of status. Since making comparisons involves others as well as one self, being able to display one's success is often an important part of making these comparisons. A champion football player may, for example, flash his Super Bowl ring. An attorney, or some other professional, will prominently display his or her professional degrees (especially if they are from prestigious schools) where others can readily see them. A military officer will show his badges of rank, and a high school athlete will often wear a letter sweater to show his or her achievements.

In most modern societies, being successful means being financially successful. That is, there are typically monetary rewards associated with being a success. As a result of this connection between success and money, people often spend a good portion of their money on unnecessary goods and services in order to visibly display their degree of success to others. This is conspicuous consumption. Clothing, vehicles, jewelry, and houses are objects which are both readily visible and can be very expensive. Consequently, these are commodities which rich people often buy and use to show their wealth - and relative success - to others. Even people who are not overly rich will sometimes sacrifice a good deal of money in order to "buy" and display some degree of status.

Finally, an end result of people being concerned with status is that communities often become *stratified*. That is, communities become divided, or stratified, into different classes (typically, higher, lower, and middle classes) based on status. As discussed in Chapter 2, taking the role of the other is an essential part of successful interaction. This occurs more smoothly when the interacting people feel more alike, or the same as, one another; and people are more apt to feel this "sameness" when they feel that they are of similar status within their community. People typically feel more at ease with one another when they feel that they are on an equal footing with each other. And when people of higher status interact with one another, their shared feeling of higher status reinforces their mutual feeling of superiority relative to people of lower status.

As a result, people - especially people of higher status - often gravitate toward others who are their status equals. They typically choose, for example, to live in proximity with others of equal status - buying homes of similar value. And, as people strive to increase their status in their community, they often elect to buy homes of ever increasing cost - engaging in conspicuous consumption. This, then, divides communities into richer and poorer neighborhoods on a sliding scale.

People also, especially those of higher status, prefer to interact with others of equal standing as they engage in recreational, civic, or otherwise "social" interaction. Again, this tends to reinforce their feelings of superiority as they mutually accept one another as being of equal and higher status and as being better than others. This interaction can take place in a variety of forms, such as joining exclusive clubs (commonly golf or country clubs), vacationing in exclusive (i.e., expensive) places, joining certain churches and civic organizations, intermarrying within a restricted group of families, and political affiliations. These activities, then, also tend to divide communities into different status groupings, and this segmentation results in creating a status hierarchy in the community. In addition, we may also note that as different status groups develop, they can develop certain differentiating characteristics. These may include different habits and patterns of speech (slang, pronunciation, etc.), and different political views - richer people being more conservative and poorer people being more amenable to social change. As these differentiating characteristics develop, they help members of the community identify one another as to which grouping they belong.

## THE LAW OF DIMINISHING RETURNS

The Law of Diminishing Returns states that when some event occurs repeatedly for an individual, the positive effects, or returns, diminish over time. Experiencing some pleasurable sensation repeatedly can even become boring. If a joint action is repeated enough - or becomes routine for an individual - the self satisfaction that comes with the successful completion of the joint action will often lose some of its effect. Routines can breed boredom. The effects of this law are often subtle but are also often quite significant.

People who have engaged in the same business or job for a long period of time and who have a routine home life sometimes go through what is called a mid-life crisis. The satisfaction that they have experienced from their professions and other parts of their life has diminished, and they feel that they have lost some of their "purpose" in life. They feel a need for a change. As a result, people may start doing a number of different things including: changing their professions, trying to get a promotion, moving, taking up a new hobby, getting religion, getting divorced, practicing yoga, starting an exercise routine, or doing volunteer work. Here, the Law of Diminishing Returns motivates people to start a new career or start a new routine in their lives; and, ultimately, the law motivates people to change or add to their definition of self.

Creativity is often a byproduct of the Law of Diminishing Returns. People will often seek a profession or hobby or some other activity which is creative in nature in order to avoid work which is too routine. Artists, writers, scientists, and engineers typically do something new and different because it is the nature of their work to *create* something new and different. Engaging in creative work is thus one way of avoiding the effects of repetition in day to day life.

The Law of Diminishing Returns can also contribute to addiction. When someone has a pleasurable experience, he or she may fall into the habit of pursuing this experience to an excessive degree. Just about any activity which is enjoyable in and of itself can become a habit; but especially when the experience involves *consuming* some substance, this habit can become addictive. Consumptive habits which can become addictive include eating, gambling, playing video games, and watching TV, as well as drinking alcohol and taking drugs. The Law of Diminishing Returns kicks in when the pleasurable experience is dulled by repetition, and the person seeks to increase the experience by consuming more. Consequently, someone pursuing an enjoyable experience can make it a habit, and a habit can become a stronger and addictive habit due to the dulling effect of repetition.

When politicians and other national leaders declare war, they need and depend on the support of the nation's people to carry out that war. Conscription is often a necessary part of getting people to march off to war; but large numbers of people often *volunteer* to go to war, especially at the outset of the conflict. One of the reasons people will volunteer like this is that going off to war offers them a break in their normal routines. To them, warfare is something of an adventure. When given the choice between (a) continuing routines that may have become dull over time and (b) risking pain, injury, and even death, millions of people have chosen the latter alternative in countless wars over the years. In this way, the Law of Diminishing Returns is a major factor in the ability of a government to sacrifice the lives of many of its people to resolve political issues with other governments.

## SAVING FACE

Whatever we are doing, we want to succeed. When we fail to achieve our goals, we can feel intense disappointment. When our failure to achieve our goals is witnessed by others, we can also experience intense embarrassment. We can be afraid that we may lose our positions of status or that others will think of us as losers. As a result, people who are very much in the public eye often go to extraordinary lengths to avoid the appearance of failure. We call this saving face.

As a general rule, we can say that the more an actor is in the public eye, the greater will be his/her efforts to avoid failure. In perhaps the most extreme examples, national leaders have often pursued losing efforts in war - beyond the point when the war could ever be won - due to a fear of losing face. Lyndon Johnson, for instance, commented to an advisor during the course of the Vietnam conflict, "I will not go down in history as the first American president to lose a war." He did so despite the fact that the continuation of the war cost many billions of dollars and lives of thousands of men without achieving victory. Ultimately, the war continued until the next presidential election, at which time Johnson chose not to run for reelection. By choosing not to run, Johnson saved face by dumping the problem of the war in the next president's (Richard Nixon's) lap.

Saving face can manifest itself in more subtle ways. In large organizations especially, people in positions of authority are often afraid to take risks or change an established course of action due to fear of failure. Most activity in large organizations takes the form of long standing and predictable routines. Changing these routines involves some degree of risk - the possibility of failure to reach some desired goal. Since others are affected by any decision to change an established routine, the people making these decisions can be reluctant to do so. Following the normal course of action is seen as the safest way to go. Here, saving face has the effect of *inaction* - people not being able to do something because of a fear of failure. Especially in the corporate world, fear of failure, and losing face, can lead to a corporation not being able to adapt to a changing business environment, and the corporation may ultimately fall behind its competitors.

In this chapter, we've looked at five motivational factors which may or may not have an effect on joint activity in various situations. When considering such factors, it is relevant to address two important questions: In what joint actions does a factor play a part? And, How does the factor affect the joint actions and to what degree?

Our human physiology gives us various needs to fulfill: food, clothing, shelter, love and companionship, and - in the case of children - nurturing. This factor leads us to start and engage in careers and routines, such as jobs and starting a family, which we deem necessary to fulfill these needs. The motivation to succeed in these careers and routines is very high since these needs are critical, in most cases, to our very existence.

Values are personal traits which help describe our selves and which we normally consider to be relevant to the successful completion of joint actions. Traits like honesty, loyalty, hard work, and compassion enable us to depend on one another and cooperate smoothly as we interact. When

*Patterns of Joint Actions*

we adhere to these values, our joint activity will more likely come to satisfactory conclusions. As we recognize others as possessing these traits, we may directly express our appreciation through compliments or indirectly by wanting to engage in further joint actions with them.

Status considerations come into play as we compare ourselves and our successes with others. The desire for higher status often motivates us in a number of ways: It leads us to pursue careers that pay more and are commonly deemed to be more prestigious than others. It motivates many of us to interact - as friends and neighbors and business associates - with people who have high status in the community. It motivates many people to avoid or shun or discriminate against those commonly understood to be of low status. A common result lies in the physical makeup of communities with people winding up living in either rich, middle class, or poor neighborhoods.

The Law of Diminishing Returns leads many people to become dissatisfied with their day to day routines. Through the numbing effect of repetition, many of us get motivated to end old careers and routines and start new ones. Creativity, divorce, and a willingness to go off to war - or other adventures - are a few of the effects of the Law of Diminishing Returns.

Finally, saving face can affect people's actions in two general ways. It can either motivate people to go to extraordinary lengths to avoid the appearance of failure in public, or it can inhibit action with the fear that change and risk might result in failure. In the first case, a small setback sometimes leads to a greater tragedy; and in the second case, inactivity can put a stop to progress and possibly endanger an individual's or an organization's long term success.

CHAPTER 5

# Types of Joint Actions

● ● ●

CATEGORIZING TYPES OF OBJECTS AND types of phenomena is a fundamental part of building a body of knowledge on any subject. When people are able to categorize and describe types of objects and phenomena, they become able to recognize and form expectations about them in different settings. Earlier, for example, we discussed two types of self-definitions (selves defined by tasks and by relationships) and the corresponding types of self-realization. These types help describe different ways people are motivated and act within different joint actions. Another example, which is a classic in sociological theory, are the four types of societal *functions* - legitimacy, integration, goal attainment, and adaptation - which, in Talcott Parsons' doctrine, need to be accommodated in any stable social system. This *typology* of functions was a cornerstone of Parsons' structural-functional theory.

Given that the joint action is the basic "unit" of social interaction, understanding different types of joint actions consequently becomes a logical way to add to our understanding of social interaction. Joint actions, obviously, can differ from one another in a variety of ways. They can vary in duration, complexity, focus, setting, and size (the number of people involved). We already made a typology of joint actions in Chapter 3 based on the way they might fit together to form patterns of interrelated joint actions. From the standpoint of the individual actors involved, joint actions could be typed as either parts of routines or careers or both. In addition, with regard to social groups, they can be either small parts of a social

*Patterns of Joint Actions*

group's network of joint activity, or they could act as a link connecting the joint actions of two different groups.

A good typology of joint actions should have two features. First, it should be universal and not particular to a single group or culture or situation. That is, the different types of joint actions described should be recognizable, or at least possible to exist, in any human society. Secondly, the typology should be instructive. Each type of joint action will have various characteristics which will set it apart from the other types. For the typology to be instructive, the observer/analyst should be able to reliably expect these characteristics to exist once she identifies a given type of joint action in a situation. This ability to *expect* certain details to be true in a situation - based on the presence of a certain type of joint action - lends predictability to the overall conceptual scheme. And predictability leads to the ability to make testable hypotheses.

In this chapter, we will focus on motivation as a criterion for building a typology of joint actions. Since the motivation and *goals* that actors have as they interact are so important, the way individuals' goals conform or "fit" together in a joint action is a fundamental way joint actions differ from one another. That is, a typology can be made - and can be instructive - based on whether the participating actors' respective goals are the same, different but compatible, or conflicting. This, of course, is not the only way to distinguish types of joint actions from one another, but it is a good place to start.

## Teamwork

When people engage in a joint action with the same goals and the same overall purpose, we often say that they form a kind of partnership with one another. Examples of partnerships are joint business ventures and successful marriages. Similarly, people engaging in "teamwork" typically do so as a result of having the same or very similar goals. That is, the definition of a team is a group of people working together to accomplish a common goal. Team sports and group recreational activities are examples of people engaging in joint actions wth the same goals. Some characteristics of this type of joint action are as follows:

Having the same goals in the joint action, the actors will probably be engaged in similar careers. That is, the joint action will likely fit into the respective "lives" of the actors in similar ways. Successfully completing the joint action and attaining the accompanying goals will likely have the same effect on the larger careers of each actor. Likewise, failure to complete the joint action successfully will probably have a similar harmful effect on the separate actors' careers.

There is usually a high degree of consensus (common understandings) in partnerships and teamwork. The actors share a common interest in the successful completion of the joint action, and they do so for the same reasons. They will perform different actions based on their mutually accepted views of their different capabilities and what "works best" in the situation. With a heightened degree of consensus, they can typically anticipate one another's actions during the joint action based largely on their ability to imagine what they themselves would do if they were in the other person's place.

As a result of this high degree of consensus, relationships are often relatively strong in this type of joint action. The actors, being aware of their common purpose, can "identify" with one another and can appreciate each other's place and actions in the situation. Strong friendships often result from these relationships. Consequently, if the joint action is part of a long term career or routine, self-realization in the joint action will rely strongly on relationship fulfillment as well as on the accomplishment of any tasks involved. That is, self-realization by relationship fulfillment and by completion of tasks will naturally coincide with one another.

Being of the same "mind", the common understandings that they rely on are less likely to be rigid or codified. Communication will be important, but it will be less concerned with "why" and more concerned with "how is the best way to get this done." Communication is more apt to be frank and direct with each actor being sensitive to, and appreciating, the point of view of the other.

Just as relationships can be strong in this type of joint action, disagreements between the actors can have serious and long term consequences.

Disagreements may arise as to the best way to complete the joint action (its plan) or as to whether or not the actors do indeed have the same goals in the situation. Unresolved disagreements can threaten the relationships between the actors and can even result in one or more of the actors feeling betrayed or personally attacked.

## CONTRACTS

A second type of joint action is one in which the separate actors have different but compatible goals. They engage in the joint action for different reasons but are still able to cooperate with one another and complete the joint action to their mutual benefit. Wth this type of arrangement between the actors, we might call this a *contract* or "exchange" type of joint action. Work related joint actions fit this type. The workers and the managers and owners in a business each have different personal goals in these situations, but they should each benefit from the successful completion of their joint activity. The workers and owners agree with one another to exchange labor (on the workers' part) for money (the owners' payback). The actors have separate goals, but they should each be realizable with their mutual cooperation. A buying and selling transaction is another example of this type of joint action. Contracts have these additional characteristics:

Having different goals, the separate actors will likely be engaged in different careers. As a result of this difference, the successful completion of the joint action will have a different effect on the careers of the different actors. And likewise, any failure in completing the joint action as planned will affect the separate actors differently.

There is less likelihood of strong relationships developing between the actors in this type of joint action; and when self-realization occurs, it will do so primarily through task completion. The separate actors are brought together for different reasons, and developing a meaningful relationship with one another is not likely to be one of them. Having said this, however, the possibility of a fulfilling relationship developing between the actors should increase if the joint actions become part of an established routine.

As pointed out in chapter two, self-realization via relationship fulfillment becomes a dominant form of self-realization when the actors are engaged in routine joint actions. This can be true even when the actors have different goals in the joint action. An example of this would be a business owner deriving satisfaction from his or her relationship with his or her employees as they work together over time.

The common understandings existing between the actors are more likely to be clearly defined before the joint actions begin and often take the form of a formalized contract. A sales contract between a home buyer and a seller is an example, as is a labor contract between a corporation and a union. Strict rules and even laws, such as fair labor laws, can also exist which may govern certain aspects of this type of interaction.

Decisions as to what actions to take in a joint action of this type will likely include something of a "cost-benefit" calculation on the actors' part. Each actor will, at least in the back of their mind, consider (1) the costs of her actions - in terms of the time and effort, or money, she expends in these actions, (2) the benefits she might expect from the others in the joint action, and (3) whether or not the expected benefits outweigh the costs. In a successful joint action of this type, each actor should realize a net benefit from their cooperative effort. As a consequence of this manner of calculation, we might not expect the separate actors to expend any more effort in their actions than is necessary to fulfill the terms of their contract. This would be in contrast to the teamwork type of joint action where the actors might be expected to exert extra effort to achieve their common goals.

A historic note - This view of people rationally exchanging costs for the sake of receiving benefits was considered by many sociologists as being the essential feature of social behavior. Borrowing concepts from economics (such as Coleman's [1990] "social capital") and B. F. Skinner's behaviorist psychology, noted sociologists including George Homans and Peter Blau created a model of social interaction called the "Exchange Theory" of social behavior. While this model was perhaps most popular from the late 1950's through the early 1960's, its origins can be traced back one hundred years to the influential German sociologist Georg Simmel. For further reading, see Homans (1958), Blau (1994), and Simmel (1907).

As the actors engage in this exchange type of joint action, each actor will likely want to get more out of the other actor than the other actor will likely want to give. Consequently, communication will often be centered around each actor's efforts to get the other to do something that the other might not want to do. The actors may negotiate with one another, cajole or flatter one another, and they may to some extent deceive one another in order to get their way in the transaction.

## COMPETITION AND CONFLICT

Joint activity such as athletic contests, political campaigns, and wars involve joint actions in which the goals of the separate actors are mutually exclusive. In competition and conflict, there are winners and losers - if one actor achieves his goal, the other does not.

The outcome of a contest or war will consequently hinder the longer term career of the loser and likely help the career of the winner. Self-realization occurs as a result of successful task completion (winning a contest, achieving victory) and rarely involves relationship fulfillment between the opposing participants.

Common understandings as to the manner in which the joint action is to take progress are typically set by some independent source or agency. In warfare, the Geneva Convention set rules and limits as to what actions are acceptable or unacceptable on the part of the combatants. In sporting contest, there is commonly a rule book, referees, and umpires to judge what are permissible actions on the playing field. Outside of these independently set rules, each side is left to their own devices.

Communication between the opposing parties is usually minimal and, when it occurs, involve a considerable and expected amount of deception. Each side will try to anticipate the other's actions and will try to counter those actions. Consequently, each side will try to hide their own communications using codes, huddles, feints, or disinformation in order to hinder the other's ability to anticipate their actions.

## Sociable Interaction

Much interaction between friends, family, and lovers does not have any concrete end result as a goal. It is interaction enjoyed for its own sake. Georg Simmel (1910) called this *sociable* interaction. Sociable interaction, as interaction for its own sake, is a broad category and takes on many forms. Common examples of sociable interaction include a dinner involving friends or family, a recreational outing, a friendly game of cards, most (nonprofessional) sports, a party, and a casual conversation.

A dominant feature of sociable interaction is that the actors *share* something between themselves. Casual conversations, for example, are joint actions in which the actors share information or joke among themselves. The sharing is based on the common understanding that the information/joke is of interest to the listener as it is to the teller. The decision-making process involved in this sharing takes the following general form: "The information is interesting to me (or I find the joke funny, etc.) and the other has similar interests (or a similar sense of humor), so I will share the information (joke) with the other." The expected result is that the other enjoys, in some manner, receiving the shared information or hearing the joke.

The common interests that exist between the actors in sociable interaction can themselves be of numerous types. And as their common interests can be of different types, so the joint actions in which they participate can differ. The actors might have a common interest in a particular professional sport, for example, and so they might discuss or watch a ball game together. If the actors have a strong common interest in politics, they may attend a political rally together or discuss the merits of separate candidate's views. Going to a movie, a concert, or play, sightseeing, bicycling, dining out, are all joint actions that people engage in together based on their common interest in the activity. As part of the interaction, the

*Patterns of Joint Actions*

actors typically share information and their attitudes and opinions with one another as these attitudes and bits of information pertain to their common interests and the activity at hand.

*Equality* is consequently the second dominant feature of sociable interaction. By having common interests, the actors are acting on a strong sense of sameness, or equality, with each other. As a consequence of this strong sense of equality between them, the actors assume themselves to be "like minded" as they decide which action is logical or appropriate to perform at any given point in the interaction.

Self-realization, here, is based on relationship fulfillment between the actors. The relationship is based on the actors perceiving their commonality or sameness with one another. Friendship in particular is based on a presumed equality between the friends. The act of sharing something which one actor finds of value, and perceiving a positive response on the part of the other, is a means of realizing this commonality with the other. As a result of the other's positive response, this interaction reinforces the actor's view of himself and gives his view of himself legitimacy. He then realizes himself. The commonality of interest between the actors reflects the commonality of selves between them. The sharing activity and the perceived end result is a way of verifying this commonality. The self is then realized based on the perceived commonality of himself with the other. The sharing creates a bond, a relationship; and the relationship is one of sameness between the actors. In this case, the common understandings which must exist to some extent in any joint action include the common understanding that the actors have common interests. They act on these common understandings by sharing attitudes and information which pertain to these interests. The feedback reinforces the legitimacy of the way they see themselves - or define their selves - in the situation.

Careers are rarely *directly* involved or affected in sociable interaction. This is true by definition. As interaction for its own sake, sociable interaction does not focus on some concrete task to be completed which would have a bearing on some greater endeavor. Sociable joint actions can be used, however, to further his or her career by what is commonly called "networking". Sociable interaction can be used as an opportunity by one actor to get acquainted with other actors and develop a network of relationships. The actor may then use this network as a means to propose, for example, some form of business activity to one of the other actors in the network. Parties, fund raising events, and golf outings are common and familiar examples of this type of networking interaction.

Sociable interaction which evolves into routines can yield strong and even life-long relationships. Since relationship fulfillment is the dominant form of self-realization in sociable joint actions, establishing a routine of these joint actions will typically result in a stronger relationship between the participants. Likewise, breaking an established routine of sociable interaction can have a detrimental effect on a relationship between friends and even lovers.

At this point, we may note that the above types of joint actions are what sociologists commonly call *ideal types*. When sociologists refer to ideal types, they are describing how some phenomena might ideally fall into different categories. For example, Max Weber discussed authority as falling into three ideal types: charismatic, traditional, and legal-rational. Social reality, however, is often complex enough to make the boundaries between different categories, or types, somewhat blurred. In everyday interaction, the criteria used to describe the different types often exist to a matter of degree or are in a complex relation to one another. The following two types of joint activity illustrate this point.

## Play

Play (Simmel, 1910) joint actions are contests (there are winners and losers) which are also sociable in nature. Games such as card games, ball games, and games of chance are examples of contests which essentially sociable in nature. The actors compete with one another, but the competition is enjoyable for its own sake, irrespective of who wins or loses. In play joint actions, the actors "test their skills" (Ibid.) and take satisfaction in

*Patterns of Joint Actions*

performing successfully in the situation. The outcome, however, does not have any effect on the actors outside of the context of the play interaction. That is, the play joint action does not exist as a part of any larger careers that the separate actors are engaged in. The consequences of who wins or loses are minimal.

Aside from games, another example of play joint actions are friendly debates and verbal "repartee". In friendly debates, the actor's goal is to make a logical point which will refute another's argument or position. The actor will gain some measure of satisfaction if she does in fact succeed in refuting the other's argument; but the joint action is often a sociable one, and the actors do not necessarily count on changing one another's minds on any particular issues. Again, the debate is a contest, but the interaction is enjoyable for its own sake. With verbal repartee, a discussion or argument between actors provides the platform for the actors to make amusing remarks, or display their wit, to the company at hand. A kind of contest ensues as the actors try to outwit one another, but the contest is rarely a serious one and creating humor is the main goal.

The modern workplace presents another situation where the line between two types of joint actions often becomes blurred. A contract exists between employers and employees whereby the employees exchange their labor for pay from the employer. Especially in workplaces where there is a strong union presence, the contract between workers and management is quite literal and specific. Employers, however, often go to considerable lengths to foster a sense of teamwork between themselves and their workers. This is done both to motivate employees to be more productive (work harder) and to facilitate cooperation between workers and their managers as they interact. Examples of the efforts to strengthen a sense of teamwork in the workplace are numerous and include the following:

A large banner hangs over the work floor at the local Post Office that reads, "Say Yes To The Goals!"

Recognizing individuals for their efforts, such as designating Employees of the Month.

Company wide get-togethers such as picnics and parties, which are intended to build a sense of fellowship between workers, managers, and owners.

Department meetings which stress a give and take between managers and their employees.

Suggestion programs by which employees suggest ways to improve conditions and efficiency in the workplace.

Surveys conducted by employers and managers designed to measure the extent to which their employees feel "engaged" in their jobs. Here, being "engaged" means to have a sense of being an important and valued part of the overall organization. An engaged employee is defined as being one who exerts extra effort beyond what is routinely expected for the sake of furthering the overall organization's goals. A survey's questions are designed to elicit the employees' opinions on various aspects of their workplace experience; and, in this case, managers can be rated as to their efforts to increase the overall sense of engagement in their workers.

At this point, we may note that this book's focus on joint actions (including types of joint actions) addresses, indirectly, a basic question in sociology: "What do sociologists study?" As human beings are so fundamentally social in nature, sociologists are presented with a wide variety of subjects and phenomena to consider. They may study types of groups, relationships, authority, communities, cultures, economies, and religions, among other subjects.

This book takes the position that the study of joint activity has relevance regardless of what area of study sociologists may pursue. Whatever social phenomenon exists that a sociologist might look at, that phenomenon is, ultimately, a product of social interaction. Any thorough understanding of social life, in any of its forms, should benefit from an understanding of how and why people do what they do as they interact with one another. This remainder of this book explores the manner in which the study of joint actions can play a meaningful role in the various aspects of sociological inquiry.

# Part II

• • •

CHAPTER 6

# An Alternative Paradigm: Joint Actions and the Study of Social Groups

● ● ●

MERRIAM WEBSTER'S DICTIONARY DEFINES (ROUGHLY) sociology as "the study of the history, development, organization, and problems of people living together in social groups". From its outset, the discipline of sociology has thus had, in one way or another, a predominant focus on social groups. For example, Emile Durkheim, one of the founding fathers of sociology, made comparisons - in 19th century Western Europe -between Catholics and Protestants and their respective rates of suicide. More recently, the influential Harvard sociologist Talcott Parsons looked at groups as they comprised structured social "systems". And up to this date, people regularly take polls and otherwise do research on various groups (say, Muslims or the rich or young people or people who voted for Donald Trump) in order to divine certain truths about them, especially when examined in comparison with other groups.

This focus on social groups exists in contrast to this book's focus on joint actions. It is the purpose of this chapter, in particular, to examine the differences between the two approaches and how they may complement one another. But before proceeding too far in this direction, it is advisable to first consider a little bit more closely how sociologists look at, and define the phrase, social groups.

## SOCIAL STRUCTURES AND SOCIAL AGGREGATES

Sociologists refer to social groups in two fundamentally different ways (Bates and Peacock, 1989), and so we may, for convenience, distinguish between and refer to these two different *types* of social groups. The first type of group consists of people who interact with one another forming a self-conscious social unit. Families, businesses, governments, schools, churches, and sports teams are all examples of this type of social group. These groups can be characterized in a number of ways. Each group typically has a name; people in these groups recognize themselves as being "members" of their respective groups; these members are aware of and agree on the group's purpose and goals; the groups typically are "structured" in that different people have different roles within them; and there is often a hierarchy among the members, with some members having more authority (and higher status) than others. Sociologists (and others, such as politicians and journalists) frequently concern themselves so much with the structured aspect of these groups that we may, again for convenience, refer to groups of this type as social structures.

The second type of social group consists of those groups of people who share some common, socially relevant, characteristic. Examples are Democrats, immigrants, conservatives, Protestants, pensioners, the unemployed, and young people. The people involved fall into some social category or other, and we may call these groups social "aggregates". The individuals in these groups do not necessarily interact with one another, and they do not necessarily think of themselves with regard to which group they are identified with.

The prevailing tendency among sociologists is to focus on groups of this second type. There a few reasons for this. The first is that, by focusing on a group with some "socially relevant" characteristic, the sociologist, or other type of researcher, is focusing on a subject which is presumed to be newsworthy, or otherwise of interest to a broader audience. The sociologist looks at a particular group because that group is noteworthy; and this, then, presumably makes the sociologist's research noteworthy. He or she may, for example, look at the religious tenents, traditions, and economic prospects of conservative Muslims (focusing on that social group) in an effort to explain the group's often extremist political views. In light of all the violence occurring around the globe, research of this type would likely be of interest to others.

Another reason sociologists commonly look at social groups of this second type is that these groups are generally amenable to statistical analysis. One group is typically compared to another group, or the general population, in terms of percentages or some other easily understood statistical measure. For example, the percentage of people who we can call middle class (the group) is steadily shrinking relative to the general population (another group), and this is taken to be an indication of a long term and important economic trend in our country.

## JOINT ACTIONS AND STUDYING STRUCTURES

When comparing the study of joint actions to the study of structured social groups (Type 1), we may note a number of interesting similarities and differences. As discussed in Chapter 3, people in Type 1 groups engage in patterns of interrelated joint actions. The group has a goal or goals, and the group's members interact in a coordinated way in their efforts to achieve these goals. To the extent that the members' actions are routine, purposefully interrelated, and authority (in larger organizations especially) is hierarchical, their joint activity takes on the appearance of being structured. In this way, the study of the group's pattern of joint activity and the study of the group as a social structure are reasonably compatible.

There are differences, however, between focusing on patterns of joint actions (hereafter referred to as the "Interactionist" approach) and focusing on groups as social structures (hereafter referred to as the "structuralist" approach). And these differences can be quite significant. First of all, interactionists focus primarily on the actions that people perform with one another, while structuralists focus more on the relationships that people have with one another. Interactionists' questions are more of the nature of, "Who is doing what and when and where and why?" Structuralists are more apt to ask, "What types of stable and persistent arrangements exist within the the group?"

Secondly, interactionists put an emphasis on communication and the emergent (Blumer, *Ibid.*) nature of interaction, while structuralists emphasize the *rights* and *obligations* of actors fulfilling *role requirements*. That is, interactionists note the importance of the communication occurring between the actors as they develop, alter, and fit their actions together. The resulting interactionist view is one that appreciates the way joint action emerges from the give and take of the actors. The structuralist view tends to see actors following more of a script as they satisfy the requirements of the roles they have in their social groups. Actors are thus seen as more creative in the interactionists' view, and their decisions as to what actions to take at any given moment are seen as potentially more problematic.

The interactionist approach suggests a more "bottom up" analysis of social phenomena, while a structuralist approach is more of a "top-down" view of social behavior. By stressing the importance of actions, interactionists tend to start any analysis with observations of what people are actually doing. From the regularities they note from these observations, they then draw conclusions which may apply to other social situations. Structuralists typically *start* with a focus on broader social contexts (social institutions, classes, and strata) and analyze them with regard to their components and characteristics. Their analyses are more a matter of examining and discussing larger wholes: their make-up and their relation to other large wholes.

Motivation is an important consideration in understanding social behavior because it is at the heart of any explanations of what *causes* people to do what they do. In the interactionist view, motivation is expressed in terms of (a) people doing what needs to be done to complete joint actions, and (b) the actors' efforts to realize their respective selves. In the structuralist view, motivation is more a matter of people conforming to social norms, values, and class interests. Structuralists see people responding to a system of rewards and punishments - conforming to other people's expectations of their behavior in order to maximize their rewards (money, sex, social approval, etc.) and avoid any possible social sanctions (fines, loss of a job, imprisonment, social ostracism, etc.). A result of this difference in views is that interactionists see motivation in more personal

*Patterns of Joint Actions*

and dynamic terms, emphasizing the self and the emergent nature of interaction; whereas structuralists see motivation as a product of broader social forces such as the society's system of norms, values, rewards, and punishments.

Finally, by directly focusing on joint actions, interactionists are better positioned to deal with the *consequences* of a group's activity. They not only look at the needs of a group, they also look at (a) the individuals' needs, (b) how the group's actions alter the disposition of the objects acted upon, and (c) ultimately how the group's actions change the overall environment in which their joint actions occur.

To briefly sum up this short section, the value of the interactionist approach comes from providing a conceptual framework to help describe the actions and nature of groups of this first type. An interactionist analysis would not just describe these actions, but would also show how these actions constitute joint actions, and how smaller joint actions fit together to create the group's greater, overall pattern of joint activity. This analysis would likely note the purpose of the group, its plan for achieving its goals, how the members' actions and joint actions fit (or fail to fit) together, critical common understandings, the members' self definitions and self-realization, its success or failure to reach its goals, and the impact of the group's activity on the environment.

## Joint Actions and Studying Aggregates

Regarding social groups of the second type, the study of joint actions may be seen as a useful tool complementing the study of social aggregates. When sociologists focus on some particular social phenomenon, it often develops as an examination of the characteristics of some social group or other. That is, sociological inquiry is typically a matter of looking at some group which is of interest to the sociologist and asking how and why that group differs from other groups.

From our paradigm, the questions of how and why such groups, or aggregates, differ from one another are best addressed using the terms and concepts discussed up to this point. In examining how groups differ, a researcher may likely compare the types of joint actions they engage in, their respective common understandings, their members' self-definitions, their goals, and how they communicate - language often being a critical difference. Researchers may also note how members of a particular group may interact (or fail to interact) with members of other groups. For example, the ability or inability to take the role of the other can be a central question when members of different groups are in contact with one another. Generally speaking, the more detail we know of the *fundamentals* of a group's social life - as these fundamentals are defined in this book - the better picture we have of that group's unique character.

CHAPTER 7

# Cause and Effect

● ● ●

FULLY UNDERSTANDING THE OCCURRENCE OF any phenomenon suggests answering the question, "Why?" *Causality* refers to questions and assertions of what causes what to happen. Statements of cause and effect address the "why" question, and they lie at the heart of any scientific theory. The realization that germs cause disease, for instance, was the essential discovery which launched the science of modern medicine. The finding that the pull of gravity causes planets to orbit the sun was central to our understanding of the solar system and to our understanding of astronomy in general. It may be argued that a body of knowledge doesn't truly become a science until valid and reliable statements of cause and effect have been established. In Norman Denzin's words (1970; p.55) "The first, and most basic test [of a theory] is a theory's ability to generate valid causal propositions; if it cannot do this, it is not a theory."

The question of causality has always been a thorny problem when referring to human behavior. Understanding why people do what they do or what caused particular events to occur has lead to a wide variety of explanations in the social sciences. These explanations have included references to psycho-analytic theory, systems of rewards and punishments, operant conditioning, class conflict, social Darwinism, and the increased role of "rationality" and bureaucracy in our lives. These are to name just a few. It's a problem not only of determining what is true and what is not, but also of determining what is important to consider versus what is merely an external manifestation of some other causal process.

Within the discipline of sociology, in particular, establishing causality has been quite troublesome. This has been largely the case because sociologists often deal with questions and phenomena which are broad in scope, such as minority and gender issues, the effects of poverty, and cultural and social change. The problem is that *people* - in large numbers, deciding what to do in their daily lives - are the immediate cause behind all social phenomena. As such, explanations concerning the cause of any broad based social condition must be reconciled with some account of why people do what they do in their daily affairs. Sometimes this problem is simply ignored, and people are hardly, if at all, mentioned in questions of causality. The explanations just focus on one social condition or social force causing another, such as poverty causing crime or the increased division of labor in modern society causing feelings of isolation and alienation.

In many of these cases, sociologists simply adopt some vague or simplified account of personal needs and behavior, borrowed from psychology or economics, which logically fits their account of why some broader social phenomenon occurs. For example, the presumed psychological "need" for social approval (praise from others and acceptance into a social group) helps explain why people adopt and conform to other people's values and conform to society's norms. This is an essential, underlying feature of structure-based theories in sociology. In the "exchange" theory of social behavior, people presumably interact based on their calculations of how much their efforts will cost them personally versus how much benefit they may expect from the other people they are interacting with. Here, peoples' decisions to interact together stem from their estimate that the interaction will yield a net profit (the reward minus the cost) to themselves personally.

But because human behavior and social conditions can be so complex, these simplistic accounts of motivation are prone to fall short. In both these cases, the theories' simplified explanations of personal behavior virtually ignore the diverse social processes within which people make decisions and perform rational acts. The result, as noted above, is that many sociologists wind up focusing on networks of social conditions and how these conditions affect one another. People become little more than a "neutral medium" (Blumer, *Ibid.*) through which these broader social conditions operate.

In this regard, the interactionist approach has an advantage because its immediate focus is on people and their actions. What people are doing is part and parcel of the language of interactionism. Here, we may note that any statement of cause and effect is a statement of a process. Whenever one thing causes something else, a process occurs. There is an initial cause and a subsequent effect and time lapses. Something happens. And interactionists make statements pertaining to processes - the process of social interaction. Consequently, these statements should be best suited to describing the processes of cause and effect in social affairs. And since the joint action is serving as our basic unit of analysis, the joint action will serve as a focal point for making statements of why people do what they do.

## Primary Causes: Making Rational Decisions

When dealing with human behavior, the most elemental cause and effect relationship is the one which describes why a person chooses to perform one particular action as opposed to any other. The "effect" is a given action. The "cause" is the reason why the actor decided to perform that action. Here, we may note that if a person performs some given action, it is either because that action was desirable in and of itself (such as eating or drinking or engaging in some sociable activity) or because the given action brought the actor closer to some desired goal. In the first case, the reason or cause behind the action is the immediate gratification the actor receives from the action. Determining the cause behind the action is simply a matter of determining how or why the action is enjoyable to the actor: He ate the hot dog because he was hungry; she read the book because she found it interesting. They had lunch together because they enjoyed each other's company.

In the second case, actions are conceived of and performed as *parts* of some larger actions. For example, writing this paragraph is a part of the larger action of writing this chapter. The chapter is written as part of writing this book, and completing this book is the ultimate goal. The fact that the smaller action is an integral part of the larger action gives the smaller action its meaning and is the reason, or cause, behind its performance. Understanding the cause behind a given action thus involves (a) understanding what the ultimate goal is that the actor has in mind and (b) understanding how the action plays a part in achieving that goal.

During social *inter*action, the goal is to complete the joint action successfully. Any individual action performed is conceived as a part of this larger whole. The individual actor performs a given action *because* he or she decides that it is necessary to the successful completion of the joint action. Therein lies the "cause" behind the action. By performing these actions and helping complete the joint action, the actors will then *realize* their respective selves as those selves are defined in the situation. This self-realization provides the emotional component - the feelings of satisfaction that come with success or the feelings of frustration that come with failure - to the actors' endeavors.

The same line of reasoning applies to determining why a person participates in a given joint action. A person does so because that individual sees that joint action as a logical part of a pattern of joint activity. The cause behind this participation lies in the joint action's logical fit within some routine, career, or group activity.

## Secondary Causes: Conditions, Factors, and Events Affecting Joint Actions

The observations made above deal with motivation as a primary cause behind a person performing one action in lieu of another. A person is motivated to perform a particular action because of its logical fit within a larger joint action. When discussing actions, however, we have previously noted that actions - whether individual or joint actions - are problematic. Any number of factors, conditions, and/or events can have a causal effect on the success or failure of a joint action. We may call these factors,

*Patterns of Joint Actions*

conditions, and events *secondary* causes affecting joint actions. They are causes which may help or hinder the progress of joint activity. We discussed five such factors in chapter four - biological needs, values, status, the Law of Diminishing Returns, and saving face. We may also refer to the fundamental components of joint actions, listed in chapter two, as a way to logically group other causes which may affect joint activity:

Actors. In order for a joint action to proceed successfully, the appropriate actors have to be available. A shortage of actors may lead to a joint action's failure, and in some instances extra actors may help and facilitate a joint action's success.

Objects. Likewise, those objects that the actors will act on need to be at hand. A shortage of objects can impede a joint action; and extra or improved objects, such as different types of tools, may help it along.

The Plan. Each joint action has a plan - who does what and when and where. This plan may be poorly conceived and, if so, may cause the joint action to fail. Conversely, an especially well conceived plan may be said to cause a joint action's success when that success would otherwise be problematic.

Common Understandings: The Facts. Rational decision making and action requires an accurate assessment of the facts of the situation. In a sense, the "facts" dictate what is the best way to achieve a desired goal. On one hand, inaccurate knowledge can easily lead to, or cause, misguided action. On the other hand, the more a person knows about a situation, the better is her likelihood to achieve success.

Common Understandings: Consensus. A joint action's success depends on the actors being in agreement as to the joint action's plan. There has to be consensus as to how they will cooperate and coordinate their separate actions in order to complete the joint action. Any condition or event which disrupts this consensus could conceivably cause a critical problem in the joint action's performance.

Communication. Effective communication is usually essential to insure that the above mentioned consensus is in place. A failure to communicate information can cause a failure in cooperation and coordination. This would be especially true whenever the actors need to adapt to changing and unexpected conditions while a joint action is in progress. On the other hand, as an example, ongoing technological innovations in communication have often had a dramatic effect in increasing productivity of large scale and complex joint activity.

Finally, a joint action's success depends on the actors successfully performing their respective individual actions. One person's failed action can lead to the actors not reaching their joint action's goals.

At this point, we might logically ask what cause and effect relationships affect *patterns* of joint action. Patterns of joint action consist of joint actions which are either interrelated or repeated or both. Briefly, we may state that if there is some failure in a joint action, then that will have an adverse effect on any pattern of which that joint action is a part. Likewise, when a joint action proceeds successfully, then the pattern of joint activity will likely proceed as planned. In any routine, career, or group activity, maintaining that activity requires the success of its individual parts. Consequently, explanations of cause and effect should focus on how well the individual joint actions are carried out and how they fit into the larger pattern of joint activity.

## History

This focus on patterns of joint activity - and the conditions and events which may affect them - puts a great emphasis on the history of the people involved in any particular social activity. It should be of little surprise that the best commentary on human events is often provided by journalists and historians. Journalists observe, record, and report on human events. As such, they are often the closest observers to what people are actually *doing* and are best positioned to note the interplay of their separate actions. Similarly, historians record and study the interplay of events. They consider how actions and events develop over time. The causes that they

*Patterns of Joint Actions*

attribute to any phenomenon typically reference what happened leading up to the phenomenon.

In the context presented here, there are historical causes behind most joint actions by virtue of the ongoing routines and long term careers in which the actors are engaged. What people are doing now will typically make sense with regard to what they have experienced in the past. When we are born, we are obviously totally dependent on others. We become involved in routines and careers (both as actors and as objects of other people's actions) from the very start. By the time we are able to make decisions and act on our own, we've all had several years of history. At whatever point in time we find ourselves, we are already involved in careers and routines and are members of some social group or other. Our personal histories determine how we see ourselves, and they consequently help shape our purpose and motivation in any given situation.

In addition to motivation, history shapes what people believe to be true in a given situation. The knowledge and "facts" that people bring to bear as they interact are gathered by learning from others and through personal experience. Individuals draw on this knowledge as they make decisions and form the common understandings necessary to the successful completion of joint actions. Accordingly, understanding what causes may be attributed to some joint action may also take into account the *origin* of any beliefs that the actors had which played a significant part in the decisions that the actors made. For example, comprehending the causes of World War I should include comprehending the process by which many Germans came to believe (commonly understand) that they were being ostracized and politically isolated by other European nations. As a general proposition, we may state the following: To the extent that common understandings affect any given joint action, understanding what causes people to perform that joint action would include understanding the historical process by which the relevant common understandings came into being.

Depending on how far a sociologist wishes to pursue questions of causality, her examination of causes and effects, routines and careers, and history may lead to further considerations. What determined the genesis of any routine or career or group? What set them in motion in the first place? What processes were involved in their formation? What event(s) changed people's beliefs - their common understandings? The *chain of causality* can conceivably reach back as far as the researcher wants. Usually it begins with some historical event which either disrupted some ongoing pattern of joint activity or or set new ones in motion or both.

## MAKING PREDICTIONS

Taking a pragmatic view, establishing statements of cause and effect and developing theories have value if they have utility. Ideas have to be useful if they are to be worthwhile and last; and concepts and ideas have utility to the extent that they help us make predictions. *Predictability* is the ultimate test of the value of any theory or set of concepts. In the realm of sociology, the best ideas are those which best describe social phenomena and can be used to help predict social behavior. If a set of ideas cannot be applied to the real world - and fails to provide concepts which which help predict what people will do - then those ideas will likely fall by the wayside in time.

As such, the interactionist approach will establish its value to the extent that it's ideas have this predictive utility. As "fundamental" concepts, most of the concepts presented here describe social interaction in very general terms and are universal - they apply to all social behavior. They can be used to help predict people's actions by sensitizing the observer as to how social interaction works (what people do when they engage in joint actions), what motivates its participants to perform particular actions (why people do what they do), what conditions must exist for the success of joint actions (common understandings, effective communication, etc.), what conditions may cause a joint action to fail, and how joint actions, as events, affect other joint actions. We've attempted to describe processes of cause and effect in social interaction, and to the extent that we understand what causes what, we may make predictions as to what is likely to occur under different circumstances.

*Patterns of Joint Actions*

In addition, we may note that predictability is, in a sense, built into the conceptual scheme presented thus far. As people engage in joint actions, they need to coordinate their respective actions as a means to successfully complete the joint action. This coordination depends on the actors being able to correctly anticipate and *predict* what each actor will do at various points of time during the joint action. This ability to anticipate and predict one another's actions in turn depends on the actors' common understandings as to the joint action's plan. To the extent that an observer has intimate knowledge of the internal workings of some joint activity, that observer should have some ability to make predictions as to the joint activity's progress. We may also note that to the extent that the observer is familiar with the ongoing patterns of joint activity, he or she should have some predictive ability as to what joint actions the actors will engage in at future points in time.

In summing up, we have separated explanations of cause and effect into three different types: primary, secondary, and historical. Explanations of cause and effect in the interactionist approach start by asking why a person decides to perform a particular action. While interacting, a person will perform a *given* action because doing so makes sense (to him or her) in whatever *joint* action he or she is participating. The action is performed as a logical part of a larger whole. If the action is not performed successfully, the larger joint action is apt to fail. In turn, a person will participate in a given joint action because doing so makes sense within the context of the larger careers, routines, and group activity in which that person is engaged. In social groups, a given joint action is performed because there is a consensus that the joint action is a necessary part of the group's overall joint activity. Again, each action, or joint action, is performed *because* the actors think of it as being a necessary part of a larger whole.

This examination of social processes in terms of how separate parts exist as parts of larger wholes represents the primary focus in comprehending causes and effects in social interaction. In addition, understanding causality in social interaction should take into account what does or does not affect the fundamental components of joint actions. Common understandings, self definitions, self realization, the disposition of objects, communication, and actors' competence all play a part in decision making and the success or failure of any joint action. Any condition or event which affects these fundamental components will cause a change in their respective joint actions, and these conditions and events should be understood and examined accordingly. In addition, factors such as values, status, diminishing returns, and saving face can directly affect joint activity by affecting the motivation of a joint activity's participants.

Thirdly, virtually all joint actions, patterns of joint actions, and common understandings have a history. Joint actions, after all, are events; and most all events have some sort of past. Key components of joint actions - self definitions, common understandings, careers, routines, and social groups - develop over time. This is often referred to as the chain of causality. The causes underlying any joint activity have origins, and these are best understood in a historical perspective.

# CHAPTER 8

# Methods and Macro Sociology

● ● ●

GIVEN THE CONSIDERABLE RANGE OF social conditions and social phenomena that human beings experience, sociologists have before them a considerable range of topics to address. A partial list of these topics include social relationships, institutions, change, conflict, migrations, attitudes, and the social divisions that exist along gender, race, religion, ethnic, and class lines. Whatever subject a sociologist might choose to study, however, that subject has to be grounded in the real world. It has to be recognizable and manifest in observable social interaction. The stance taken here is that this observed social interaction is best described in the terms and concepts so far presented in this book. As such, the study of joint actions could, or should, logically play a part in the study of any social phenomena.

At this point, however, we may note that it remains a considerable task to merge the study of joint actions to the study of "macro" social conditions and events. That is, most sociologists concern themselves with conditions and events that occur or exist on a very large scale. The topics listed above are testament to this fact. The study of the fundamentals of social interaction, however, is generally thought of as "micro" sociology - a distinctly separate subject. In the mindset of many sociologists, immediate and observable social interaction appears to be far removed from the broader social "forces" at work in society - and they consider interaction to be a *consequence* of these forces. The purpose of this chapter is twofold: first, to discuss the methods researchers might use to study joint activity and then to present an argument as to how to apply knowledge of joint activity to the study of macro-social phenomena.

## Six Questions: Who, What, When, Where, How, and Why

Joint actions are events. As such, the study of joint actions, and patterns of joint actions, assumes its own particular character. They involve answering the questions who, what, when, where, how, and why.

"When" and where" are straight forward enough questions. Answering them simply locates the subject social interaction in time and place. Answering the question "who" identifies the people engaged in the interaction, but necessarily includes determining the subject individuals' self definitions. Determining these self definitions should include describing how these selves are defined in terms of any relevant tasks to perform and relationships to fulfill in the joint activity.

"What" should be answered, again, in terms of what joint actions make up the social interaction in question. Answering this question will involve descriptions of the joint actions and their overall goals.

"How" refers to the *plan* of action for each joint action, or how the actors fit their individual actions together to complete the joint actions in question. The plan, of course, consists of common understandings held by the participating actors, and so describing these common understandings plays a part in knowing how the actors go about their joint activity. Depending on the depth of analysis, describing the plan may include a detailed listing or diagram of these individual actions and commentary on how each action contributes to accomplishing the overall joint action. "How" also includes describing how the actors communicate with one another and how they adapt to changing circumstances as the joint actions progress toward their conclusions.

Answering the question "why" amounts to addressing cause and effect relationships as discussed in the previous chapter. People perform individual actions because of their logical fit (from the actor's perspective) within a larger joint action. People engage in joint actions because of their perceived fit within larger patterns of joint activity. People reconsider and adjust their actions due to changing and evolving conditions and events. Answering the *why* question then becomes a matter of gathering as much information as possible about the fundamental components of these joint actions and patterns of joint actions.

## METHODS

**Participant Observation**. Answering the questions who, what, when, where, how, and why can involve a number of different research techniques, or methods. The method most closely associated with the interactionist perspective is *participant observation*. Participant observers are people who get as close as they can to the actions being studied. Ideally, they are actual participants in the joint actions in question. By being close to the interaction, participant observers are in a position to be aware of most, if not all, of the relevant components of the joint actions being studied. This would include the common understandings assumed by the actors, the actors' respective self definitions, their modes of communication, how the actors coordinate their actions to complete joint actions, etc. This involvement in the totality of the joint actions is especially important since the progress of any joint action is affected by a number of these different components. A classic study, making use of participant observation, is Howard Becker's *Outsiders: Studies in the Sociology of Deviance* (1973). In this book, he - as a saxophone player - describes participating in the world of jazz musicians (including their drug use) in Chicago in the 1940's. And by doing so, he was further able to make relevant observations as to how these people became a group of "outsiders".

In the best case, the participant observer is able to anticipate and predict the actions of other actors. That is, as people rely on common understandings of their mutual situation in order to properly anticipate one another's actions, the participant-observer's ability to understand and anticipate what will happen in a given situation gives him or her, to some extent, the capacity to make predictions concerning the *type* of interaction observed. This, in turn, may give the observer the opportunity, in some circumstances, to make generalizations regarding that type of interaction and, ultimately, test hypotheses.

Aside from participant observation, sociologists use a number of different tools and methods to gather data. These include interviews, personal histories, documents, historical records, surveys, video and audio recordings, census, and other sources of aggregate data. While it is beyond the scope of this book to debate in detail the pros and cons of using these various tools, it may be worthwhile to list a few of them and make a few observations on their utility in researching joint activity.

**Video and Audio Records**. Video and audio equipment may be used to unobtrusively produce records of people's actions. Their advantage is that, under favorable circumstances, they can produce a picture of what people are doing that is both detailed and easy to review. Their limitation is that they provide little direct information as to the actors' common understandings, self definitions, and their "plan" of action in the situation. They also do not provide information as to how any joint action recorded fits into any greater pattern of interrelated joint actions.

**Interviews and Histories**. Interviews and personal histories (such as diaries and autobiographies) are best suited for providing information pertaining to individual actors' goals and the rationale they used to achieve those goals. They can provide insights into what the actors were thinking and were aware of as they decided to perform one action as opposed to others in various situations. Interviews and personal histories can also be used to show how an actor's participation in specific joint actions fit into his or her personal career(s) and into ongoing routines. A disadvantage to using these methods is that the accounts that people give of their own actions are produced after the fact and may not be totally accurate. The descriptions that people give of their actions are often skewed to be in conformity with currently accepted understandings as to what actions are appropriate to perform in the situations in question. Likewise, the reasons, or motivations, that they offer may be expressed in such a way as to show themselves in the best light. Typically, a person will say that he did

*Patterns of Joint Actions*

what was the most logical thing to do given the overall plan of the joint action in question. This account may not include some motivational factor related to some ongoing personal career in which the actor is engaged. C. Wright Mills discussed this dilemma in his classic essay "Situated Actions and Vocabularies of Motive" (Mills, 1940).

As discussed in the previous chapter, a thorough understanding of social interaction involves understanding the historical context in which the interaction took place. Historical records can often provide relevant information as to the causes affecting joint activity by helping to illustrate this historical context. These sources may include journalistic accounts of events, descriptive essays, biological information, and legal documents to name just a few. The information from these sources will be relevant to the extent that they help describe the routines, careers, common understandings, and group activity that all help shape the motives and methods of the subject actors. The general point is that any analysis of some specific joint activity should include a picture of how that joint activity came into being in light of the events and circumstances leading up to it - and historical documents and records may help reveal just what these events and circumstances were.

**Surveys and Polls**. Surveys and polls are perhaps the most popular research instruments used by sociologists. They are typically questionnaires given to a sample of some population in order to determine how different social "variables" (such as education, income, gender, family structure, beliefs, attitudes, and activities) correlate with one another within that population. For example, if a survey showed that people who have higher income also tend to vote Republican, the researcher would conclude that there is a correlation between the two variables. He or she would then be left with the task of explaining the connection between them - why or how one affects the other.

For the analysis of social interaction, surveys can have a significant, though limited, value. They may be useful by providing a "snapshot" (Denzin, 1969) of a group of subjects, yielding data which can give a picture of a population of people but which is frozen in time and place.

This snapshot can help describe many of the correspondents' common understandings (beliefs, how they think of themselves, and what they think of others) as well as other personal information (age, sex, education, etc.) which may be useful to a researcher. However, the interactionist's main focus is on what people are *doing* and why. This type of data is often more difficult to obtain using surveys and questionnaires due to the fact that questionnaires typically employ closed-ended questions while open-ended questions are more suitable to finding out what people are doing. Consequently, a questionnaire would have to be carefully crafted to produce information on many of the fundamental components of the respondent's interaction with others. This would include what joint actions they engage in, their careers and routines, who they interact with, and the *situational* common understandings they employ as they interact.

In addition, surveys are poor instruments for gathering at data on the *process* of social interaction. Key features of interaction are difficult if not impossible to capture using close-ended questions. These include communication, how the participants fit their actions together, how the participants adapt to changing circumstances, and how the participants realize or fail to their selves in various joint actions. These factors are critical to the progression of joint actions but which cannot be addressed adequately with fixed questions and limited responses. While surveys may be able to provide a reasonable snapshot of their respondents, a good analysis of social interaction requires something more akin to a motion picture.

**Statistics**. Like surveys, statistical data such as census figures do not directly illustrate social interaction, but they often provide information which indirectly sheds light on patterns of joint activity. Census data often supplies figures pertaining to the outcomes or products of social interaction. For example, unemployment statistics are an outcome which help show how successfully businesses, and the economy, are operating over time in a given population. Statistical measures can be especially valuable since since they are often gathered periodically - they can provide critical clues as to how patterns of interaction are changing over time. Used in this

*Patterns of Joint Actions*

way, statistics can help create a "moving picture" of long term routines, careers, and social groups.

Regardless of the methods used, the point is to gather as much reliable information as possible - from whatever source - in answering the questions who, what when, where, how, and why. Depending on the resources available to the researcher, it's perfectly reasonable to use more than one method in an analysis. This is occasionally called *triangulation* (Denzin,1970). Each of the fundamentals of interaction has a somewhat different character, and researchers may find that different methods are best suited for gathering data on each one of them. Video and audio recordings may be best suited for witnessing discrete actions. Participant observation may be best for determining what common understandings are relevant to a joint action's plan. Surveys may be best suited for gathering information on long term routines. Historical records may best reveal those conditions and events which alter patterns of joint actions. Interviews may be the best approach to determining the nature of actors' self definitions and careers.

In addition, as researchers triangulate their data, they may use one method to confirm or refute data gained from another source. For example, interviews may be used to confirm or challenge data concerning common understandings gathered from participant observation. This "cross checking" procedure could serve as a useful means for validating and adding credibility to any analysis of the data.

## INTERACTIONISM AND THE STUDY OF MACRO-SOCIAL PHENOMENA

The question may still linger as to just how the interactionist approach can be relevant to the study of large scale social phenomena. The applicability of the interactionist approach in "macro" sociology lies in three characteristics of its concepts.

First, as mentioned at the beginning of this chapter, interactionist concepts are grounded in the real world. They make direct reference to what people are doing. In the analysis of any social phenomenon, whether micro or macro in scope, describing what people are doing (or have done) should be an essential element of that analysis. For any social phenomenon to have any relevance at all, it has to be recognizable and manifest in observable social interaction. And the best way to describe that interaction is in terms of the joint activity that the subject people are engaged in. This description would include references to their careers, routines, common understandings, the success or failure of joint actions, the joint actions of groups, etc.

Secondly, many regularities exist in social interaction. People have similar needs and often live in similar circumstances. They consequently often develop similar goals and careers, they fall into similar routines, and they develop certain common understandings as to the nature of their circumstances. Joint actions and patterns of joint actions often have broadly recognizable differences and similarities. This fact provides a basis for comparing and contrasting different social groups to one another. People in one segment of a population will often engage in routines and careers and develop common understandings which are noticeably different from those of another segment of the population. With the terms and concepts presented thus far, it becomes possible to identify different parts of a society based on the different *characteristics* of joint activity which can be associated with each part.

Thirdly, many joint actions themselves occur on a macro scale. To the extent that studies of large institutions and organizations are relevant to a researcher, these organizations are best viewed with regard to the joint actions they perform. For example, a study of the Industrial Revolution might include a description of US Steel; and US Steel operated as a huge joint action utilizing a developing technology and involving thousands of people interacting with one another for the ultimate purpose of creating wealth. Governments, large educational institutions, revolutionary groups, and churches - as well as corporations - all operate as large complex joint actions, and they should be analyzed accordingly.

Likewise, many socially significant events occur as very long and involved joint actions. World War II was such an event. It lasted six years and involved the lives, at one point or another, of most of the people on the planet. The women's suffrage movement, the 2016 Presidential election, and the Russian Revolution were all macro events that occurred as greater joint actions; and as joint actions, they can be studied and understood in terms of those fundamentals which apply to all joint actions.

At this point, we may briefly look at a classic sociological study for an example of how interactionist concepts can be applied to an analysis of macro-social phenomena.

## THE PROTESTANT ETHIC AND THE SPIRIT OF CAPITALISM REVISITED

In his famous sociological analysis, Max Weber (1904) cited a causal relationship between a distinct ethic and the rise of modern capitalism in sixteenth and seventeenth century Western Europe. Without going too deeply into the complexities of Weber's analysis, the Protestant Ethic represented a set of religious beliefs that helped spur the development of capitalistic enterprises. The religious beliefs were common understandings - within various Protestant sects - about God, man, and the relationship between the two. The common understandings included the following beliefs:

That people were "predestined", from birth, for either eternal salvation or eternal damnation upon death, and that they could not alter their own individual outcomes.

That people had a "calling" in life - a religious duty to perform.

That people should refrain from material, "this worldly" concerns in life in favor of more aesthetic, "other worldly" concerns. Their main focus should be on religious matters and ultimately the afterlife rather than on their immediate comforts. This was a central characteristic of acting in accord with one's calling.

While people could not control their eternal destiny, success in their works could be taken as a sign that they were fulfilling their religious calling and that they were indeed among God's elect.

Wealth acquired through industry, then, was taken to be a sign of of God's favor. But since spending it could be sinful, the accumulation of wealth became a religiously inspired goal. This goal was in contrast to the more ordinary goal of acquiring wealth in order to simply buy more goods and services.

With this new type of goal, careers and routines changed. At the time of the Reformation, many people conducted business, and capitalism existed on a relatively small scale. But with the goal of accumulating wealth without spending it on luxuries, business activity acquired a new and more heightened energy. Since the ultimate goal was to create wealth as a sign of fulfilling one's calling, Protestants reinvested their earnings into their enterprises rather than spending them. Reinvesting profits became part of the plan and routine of conducting business. This became the new Spirit of Capitalism, and businesses grew and prospered because of it.

The argument, here, is that the cause and effect process is best understood in terms of the fundamentals of social interaction. This is true even though the phenomenon occurred on a large scale. Changes in common understandings (about man and God) caused a change in people's definitions of their selves and, consequently, their goals and careers and routines and the joint activity they engaged in. These changes occurred in a similar way for a large number of people in a broad area of Europe. As a result of these similarities, we can discuss and understand this broad social change in terms of the fundamentals which are the foundation of all social interaction.

In the case of The Protestant Ethic and the Spirit of Capitalism, social change occurred when common understandings (the Ethic) affected economic joint activity - Capitalism. There are, of course, other ways social change occurs, and these may also be discussed with reference to the fundamentals of joint actions. This is the subject of the following chapter.

CHAPTER 9

# Social Change

● ● ●

IN CHAPTER 7, OUR FOCUS was on cause and effect relationships, asking *why* people perform one action as opposed to any other and what the consequences are when those actions are performed. An additional logical step is to consider how joint activity and patterns of joint activity change over the long term and across society. At this point, we can examine the causes of social change. Social change is, of course, a very broad topic, and its causes can be varied and complex. Given the perspective presented in this book, with its emphasis on joint actions and patterns of joint actions, there are a number of observations we can make on the subject.

## CHANGE AS INEVITABLE

First of all, we may note that change is inevitable. In every action that we perform, some change occurs. This is true by the very definition of the term "action". Any rational action is done in order to change something, otherwise there would be no point in doing that action in the first place. In addition, all actions are directed toward some object or other, and that object is either created, transformed, repositioned, or destroyed whenever someone acts on it. The result is some alteration of the environment - things are not the same as they were before the action took place. And, of course, acting is a part of life. People cannot *not* act. We all must perform some actions to satisfy some need or other every day, even if it is no more than doing something to avoid boredom. Finally, when people *interact,* they are directly affecting - or changing - one another's actions. Again, this is true by definition. Even when people perform a routine joint action, they are reaffirming and reinforcing their common understandings of how people *should* interact in that particular type of joint action. This alone has a consequence in future joint actions of that type. People simply cannot interact without altering one another's behavior.

## DEFINING *SOCIAL* CHANGE

Also, it is proper to define *social* change. Individuals change naturally enough. They mature, learn, progress along various careers, change the way they interact with others, grow old, and eventually die. *Social* change, as the phrase is commonly used, occurs when the lives of a large number of people change in a similar way, and the change has an effect across generations. The more traditional sociological account of social change is to describe it as a change in a society's "structure". In this book, social life is presented as the sum total of joint actions which people perform with one another as they go about their daily (or weekly, monthly, or yearly) routines and as they strive to progress in their various careers. Widespread social change occurs and is noticeable when these careers and routines and other patterns of joint actions change in a significant and similar way for a large portion of a population.

Another way to put this is to note that many or most people in a population engage in similar patterns of joint actions. People's families, their work, their beliefs, their routine are typically stable and have a familiar character within the population. At times, conditions change and events occur which affect these stable patterns of joint activity in the same way for many people. This would be social change. The position presented her is that the fundamentals of social interaction are the proper focus of any analysis of social behavior. Accordingly, both the manifestations of social change and its causes can best be examined in these terms.

Since change is inevitable, the question is not if social change will occur but *how* change will occur. While the process of social change may take on a wide variety of forms, we may consider the causes of change in terms of a few broadly defined categories: changes in the environment, large organizations, innovation and imitation, widespread failures of careers and/or routines, and changes in common understandings.

## Sources of Change

**Environmental Change.** As noted above, changes in the environment are inevitable. People are always performing one action or another, and whenever they do so, some change, however slight, occurs. Change is most notable and significant when a large portion of the population performs the same, or similar, actions - the sum of which changes the environment on a large scale. Global warming is an example of change in this manner. When one person burns fossil fuel, the effect on the environment is so small as to be unnoticeable. But when billions of people perform the same action for hundreds of years, the effect on the environment can be devastating.

Once the environment changes in a significant way, patterns of joint activity may be disrupted, and people may be forced to follow new careers and routines and form new groups to meet the changing circumstances. For instance, history is replete with examples of people engaging in mass migrations due to changes in the environment - often as a result of over population in some area. The peoples of Europe and North America are largely descendants of people who migrated, many centuries past, from Asia. The change in the environment was the increase in the number of people in a limited area. This circumstance induced many tribes to move westward in search of new areas to settle. Presently, many peoples are migrating from Africa and South Asia to Europe and from Latin America to the U.S. and Canada for similar reasons.

**Innovation and Imitation.** Whenever a person decides to act in one way as opposed to any other, that person makes the decision based on what he or she thinks is the best course of action to take in order to gain their desired result. This is the basis of rational decision-making. When a person thinks of a *better* way to achieve an end in some activity, we call it innovation. Innovations change *how* joint actions are performed - they change a joint action's plan. When a person creates a new device to use to help achieve an end, the innovation is called an invention. Employing the invention represents a new and better way to do something. And when there are new and better ways to do things, those innovations are frequently imitated by others who engage in similar joint actions and who have similar goals. Innovations can thus become instruments of social change to the extent that large numbers of people engage in similar routines and careers and will alter their activity when presented with new and better ways to get things done. For example, double-entry bookkeeping, developed in the sixteenth century, was an innovation which aided merchants and other businessmen as they kept their accounts. This helped the spread of capitalism. Computers and motor driven vehicles are just a couple of obvious inventions whose use on a great scale have altered the lives of virtually all of us.

**Large Organizations.** In many instances, large organizations are agents of social change through their ability to direct and coordinate the actions of a large number of people. Large corporations can effect change by employing people and providing the public with desired goods and services. This usually results in raising the overall standard of living for a society. Governments are groups with the power to directly change people's actions across a whole nation. Taxation, conscription, war making, and certain legal requirements (such as requiring a driver's license) compel people to engage in joint activity that otherwise they would not. Other laws designate certain actions as being illegal, which restricts certain types of joint actions. Public works projects and government subsidies, such as grants, have the effect of generating new joint activity - creating new careers and routines. Large organizations also effect change through competition and conflict. Governments will make war, trying to inflict their will on the people of other nations; and multinational corporations compete with one another, often affecting the economic activity of more than one society.

*Patterns of Joint Actions*

**Widespread Failure in Patterns of Joint Actions.** When previously discussing cause and effect relationships, we briefly noted that if there is some failure in a joint action, then that will have an adverse effect on any pattern of which that joint action is a part. At times, failure in patterns of joint actions can be widespread and cause far reaching social change. This can happen in two different ways. First, if many people are frustrated in their efforts to reach similar goals, they may develop a collective awareness of their mutual frustration and try to do something about it. They may thus form organizations, coordinating their efforts to effect change. Labor unions, religious groups, political parties, and revolutionary groups are examples of such organizations. The Pilgrims, being frustrated in exercising their religious beliefs in Europe, banded together, emigrated, created the "Mayflower Compact", and played a large part in the development of America. Revolutions have changed the political landscape in many countries, and labor unions have worked to change and improve the economic makeup of most modernized nations.

Secondly, when there is a failure within a greatly interconnected pattern of joint actions, the entire pattern may come under considerable stress or collapse. Lack of success in one part of the pattern can have a ripple effect on the whole network of joint activity. This has occurred numerous times in different economies. Businesses have become more and more linked to one another as production, financing, marketing, and distribution have become more complex, specialized, and interdependent. This is ever more the case as economic activity has become more global in scope. For example, when there is a threat that a government may default on its bonds, even in a small country like Greece, the effect may be felt half way around the world.

**Changes in Common Understandings** represent perhaps the most subtle, interesting, and far-reaching sources of social change. Any action we perform relies on an estimation of the likely results of that action. And that estimation is based on our understanding of how things "work" in the world. We base our actions on our knowledge of our environment - the nature of the objects around us. When our common understandings of how things work change in a significant way, our actions, our interaction, and even our society can change as a result.

Most of the objects we deal with are tangible, and so most of what we know about our environment is based on physical evidence. By being tangible, we can see, hear, and feel them. They are relatively constant, and we know them through direct experience with them. Our actions toward tangible objects typically yield predictable results; and these actions, in turn, have the quality of becoming fairly routine.

Other objects are not so easily known. Some physical objects are of such proportions that we cannot experience them directly. The Earth looks flat but is actually round. Its size is such that our senses are deceived as to its true nature. Other objects are intangible and exist in the abstract. Space, character, "proper" behavior, Christianity, health, stylish dress, patriotism, love, honor, and evil are objects which we may act upon or which affect our actions, but how we define them is not so clear cut. With these objects, people largely adopt others' definitions of the objects as their own. But since these definitions are not so fixed, they can - and often do - change. And when they do change, we also change our actions with regard to them.

Accordingly, changes in common understandings concerning the nature of significant objects are often the source of significant social change. For example, when people came to realize that the Earth was round instead of flat, considerable social changes were set in motion. New worlds were discovered, new trade activity arose, new wealth was created, slavery flourished, migrations occurred, and new tensions (and wars) arose between nations. As another example, the Protestant Reformation - and all the subsequent change that went along with it - was based on disputes pertaining to prevailing understandings about God, man, salvation, and the role of the Church.

Perhaps the most significant way changes in common understandings become sources of social change involves changes in our understandings of ourselves and each other. The way we interact relies heavily on these self and other definitions. Routines, careers, and other patterns of joint actions become set in large part based on these definitions. And when these definitions change among large numbers of people, so will extensive patterns of joint activity.

As an extended example of this, we may look at our Declaration of Independence. The understanding that "....all men are created equal and are endowed with certain unalienable rights ... " has played a great part in social change. This understanding helped launch our war of independence and helped determine how we govern ourselves. Our joint actions with one another are heavily influenced by this underlying belief that, as we interact, we are essentially equal to one another as opposed to being different. Our system of laws and even notions of common courtesy rest on our beliefs in equality and individual rights. And the fact that "all men" only referred to a limited segment of the population at the time (white adult males) has been a source of contention, confrontation, and change ever since the words were written.

As another recent example, the conflict between certain Islamic groups and Western peoples has, as a cause, the common understanding (among Westerners) that women should have rights that are equal to those of men. Globalization has had an effect of increasing the amount of interaction between previously far flung peoples. As Muslim men note that Muslim women are having more contact with Western ideas, many fear for their own identities. They may fail to realize their selves to the extent that their selves are defined via their more traditional relationships with their wives, sisters, and daughters. That is, joint actions and relationships between men and women in most Islamic societies are based on definitions of men being superior to women and having more rights than women. Their violent reaction to Westerners is largely an attempt to resist this change in understandings that women are equal to and should have equal rights as men. And the extensive violence of current conflicts is evidence of the degree to which changes in common understandings can contribute to widespread change and conflict.

At this point, then, it is worthwhile to examine the *process* by which widespread changes in common understandings of socially significant but *intangible* objects occurs. This is especially significant when dealing with changing definitions of ourselves and others and how we are to interact with one another.

Our common understandings of intangible objects are largely gained as a matter of "popular beliefs". They are typically adopted from others, and their definitions and meanings are a matter of widespread consensus. Being a matter of popular belief, then, changes to these beliefs are typically met with resistance. As a result, when changes in common understandings do occur, they often take a number of steps. In many cases, these steps may be summarized as follows:

A number of people realize that they have some common beliefs and goals which run contrary to prevailing common understandings and practices. As a result, these aggrieved people collectively endeavor to change the existing beliefs.

Through various actions, these people purposefully make their alternative views known to others. First, they often present an argument which is logically linked to a broader understanding that is accepted by others. In many cases, the belief that they are promoting is presented as *part* of a greater truth. For example, if people generally accept - as stated in our Declaration of Independence - that all men are created equal and have certain unalienable rights, then why are some groups legally discriminated against? This was a logical argument presented in the American Civil Rights movement.

The aggrieved people then typically endeavor to broadcast their argument to the general public. They take actions such as making speeches, public demonstrations (either nonviolent or violent or both), newspaper opinion pieces, sermons, blogs, or (in Martin Luther's case) nailing their grievances to a church's door to make their point.

When a significantly large number of people in a community adopt a new common understanding, others with whom these people interact will be more likely to accept the new understanding to be true. That is, if *enough* people share the same understanding, individuals who are in contact with these people take that as evidence that the new understanding

*Patterns of Joint Actions*

is indeed a fact. At this point, the new understanding will spread as if it has a life of its own. A mutually reinforcing cycle develops as some people spread the belief to others, increasing the number of people possessing the belief, which then increases the likelihood that the belief will spread to even more people. The point at which the new understanding starts to feed on itself and spread at an ever increasing rate is called the "tipping point" (Gladwell, 2002).

The change in common understandings regarding the War in Vietnam during the 1960's provides a good case in point of this process. First, the war was supposed to end quickly and successfully. The United States had the most powerful military, and their cause - fighting Communism - was considered just. But victory was not quickly realized; and slowly people, especially *young* people, realized a new way of looking at the conflict. They argued that the war and its violence was unjust, not winnable, and they protested vigorously against it. This new view took hold, in its early stages, in large part because the protesters were in close physical proximity with one another and in the midst of a growing segment of the population - college and university students.

Attitudes toward the war changed ever so slowly until 1968 when even the mainstream media, such as Time magazine and the CBS Evening News, adopted an anti-war posture. At this point, anti war sentiment grew at a greater pace, and the politicians chose to wind down the conflict. The main reason the war continued to drag on as long as it did was because of America's leaders' fears of losing face by admitting defeat.

In the realm of style and fashion, changes in common understandings largely start with the Law of Diminishing Returns. When we change our attitudes toward something, we usually do so because we think that the *new* attitude is better than the old one. That is an underlying facet of rational action - we do something because we decide that the end result will be better than what previously existed. As people plod along in repetitive activity, the Law of Diminishing Returns makes many of us dissatisfied with existing routines, and we seek change. When individuals see others doing something new, they may decide that others changed because the newer way is better than the what was older and established. If enough people adopt this newer attitude, the effect of the tipping point gradually takes hold, and the new way eventually becomes the norm. Changes in hair styles, dress, and manner of speech typically follows this pattern.

The most interesting and challenging aspect of understanding social change is that the five sources of change discussed above rarely occur in isolation. The cause and effect relationships involved in change are almost always complex. And when change occurs, it often happens that all five sources of change play a part. We may look at the rise of the Nazis in Germany in the 1920's and 30's as a case in point:

History. The Germans had lost World War I, being humiliated as a people, and were suffering economically under the onerous terms of the Treaty of Versailles. This, we may say, was the environment Germans faced in the 1920's. Global economic activity worsened in the late 20's with Germans, especially, experiencing a horrific period of hyperinflation. The extended pattern of economic interaction was failing.

At this time, Adolph Hitler started making speeches blaming Jews for Germany's misfortunes and promoting the belief that Germans, as Aryans, were racially superior to other peoples. He and others created the National Socialist Party, an organization which steadily grew in size and became quite effective in organizing rallies, staging parades, and intimidating opposition groups such as the Communists. Much of their organization was active in spreading propaganda using innovations such as amplifying sound equipment (used in rallies), telephones (to help co-ordinate joint actions), radio, and eventually motion pictures. Through these efforts, and the fact that most Germans continued to suffer economic hardships, more and more Germans accepted the Nazis' set of beliefs as their own. These included the causes of Germany's misfortunes, its rightful place in the world, and its impending greatness. The Nazis' organization helped, in many cases, put people to work and overall raised their feeling of self worth. As people increasingly identified with the Nazi cause, Hitler came to power in a relatively short period of time.

In this instance, all five sources of social change were in play. Patterns of interaction were failing, creating changes in the economic environment; a large organization (the Nazi Party) was created to effect change; innovations were employed; and concerted efforts were successfully made to change people's common understandings of themselves and others. In fact, we may see these five sources of change interconnected with one another to form a *pattern* of change. Failure in patterns of interaction and environment give birth to new understandings as to the causes and effects related to failures. This then leads to people organizing efforts to change others' understandings of themselves and others, and eventually a majority of people form new ways of addressing problems and interacting with one another.

## PREDICTING THE WEATHER.

When meteorologists generate a weather forecast, they feed weather related data into a computer's database and process that data using extremely sophisticated software. The instruments they use for their measurements are relatively simple - thermometers, barometers, hydrometers, etc. The data these instruments produce is easy to fathom - temperature, air pressure, precipitation, wind speed and direction are all concepts most people understand. But the amount of data is so huge, the calculations that the computers make are so numerous, and the software is so complex, that only the most advanced computers can handle the task. This is the case because so much is happening at the same time. While the Earth is spinning and revolving around the sun, temperatures are changing, jet streams are shifting, air masses are moving, and water is constantly evaporating and falling from the sky. All these changes are occurring simultaneously, and they affect one another. Predicting the weather necessitates having an understanding - a "model" - of how these different events interact. The accuracy of any forecast largely depends on how well the model "understands" cause and effect relationships in the measured weather conditions. The more accurate and complete the data, and the more valid and reliable the model, the more detailed and accurate will be the meteorologist's predictions.

Predicting social change may eventually evolve into a similar type of analysis. Foremost of all, predicting change will require knowing as much as possible about what people are doing. This, again, will largely be a matter of knowing what joint actions people are engaged in, their nature, and how these joint actions form patterns of joint actions. In large part, predicting change will rely on monitoring any changes in the beliefs (common understandings) which people hold and rely on when making decisions. Statistical tables, such as employment statistics, housing, and statistics related to the family, give clues as to how patterns of activity are changing. Periodic surveys asking questions about respondents' day to day actions may provide indications of shifts in a population's routines. The same or similar surveys may yield a picture of a population's beliefs, their goals, how people plan on achieving these goals, and how these goals may be changing - that is, changes in people's careers. Returning to a previously used metaphor, sociologists may utilize a variety of these methods to create as many "snapshots" as possible of what people are doing, and why, at different points in time. With enough data, these snapshots may then be put together to create a motion picture of what people are doing, how their beliefs are changing, and how joint activity is changing, in a given society.

Census figures provide a simple example of how broad statistical data can help create a moving picture of widespread change. In 1967, roughly 28% of the full time workforce in America was female. This was also (roughly) the time of the beginning of the women's liberation movement. By 2009, the percentage of the workforce which was comprised of women grew to 43%. Also, from 1957 to 2010, the birth rate (births per woman) halved, from 3.8 per woman to 1.9. These figures help show how the understanding that women are as capable as men and deserve equal rights - in the family and in the economy as well as by law - is having a huge impact on our society.

*Patterns of Joint Actions*

Once sociologists have a reliable picture of how societies are changing, and have changed in the past, they may then turn to predicting how change may occur in the future. This may be done in two different ways. First, they may look at different pictures of social change and then generalize as to what *types* of change may be associated with different types of social conditions. Again, for a simple example, widespread economic failure (a type of condition) has repeatedly lead to political change. Whenever this type of condition occurs, we may then expect some degree of political change to occur at a future time.

Secondly, a picture of ongoing social change may be projected into the future to predict how these changes will affect the broader society further in time. For example, as noted above, more women are entering the workforce and procreating less. This may lead us to expect a number of continuing changes in the broader society. Average family size will likely continue to shrink, and working parents will rely more and more on extended family members to help in child rearing. Also, income inequality will likely continue to grow due, in part, to the growing number of DINKs in our society. DINKS (Double Income, No Kids) are couples who both have careers and who do not feel the need to become parents. With double incomes and fewer expenses, these households have relatively higher incomes. This in turn contributes to a continuing tendency in our society to "spread out" economically. While DINKs gravitate toward the higher end of the economic scale, there are also more working mothers without partners who are stuck with low paying jobs and higher expenses (particularly day care) and find themselves nearer the bottom of the economic order.

Of course, creating motion pictures of change and using them to predict future change suggests a monumental degree of effort, and perhaps cooperation, on the part of researchers. But with the advent of the Information Age, with the Internet providing new and unprecedented access to huge amounts of data, this approach should become more and more viable.

# CHAPTER 10

# Other Concepts

● ● ●

IN ANY UNIFIED THEORY, THE concepts which comprise that theory must be logically related to one another. This interrelationship is typically accomplished by having some central idea, or ideas, specifying what the focus of the theory is - just what are the primary objects of the analysis; what exactly are the theorists studying. Once these primary objects are established, other concepts tend to "fall into place". Their relevance exists to the extent that they help describe and explain these primary objects. For example, one of the chief attractions of Parsonian theory was that it clearly defined its central focus - it was a theory about social systems. Other concepts, such as those related to norms, values, roles, and functions, were important as they helped describe what social systems were all about. The fact that Parsons provided some order to the ideas of many different sociologists lent credibility and popularity to his theoretical approach.

In the preceding chapters, we have discussed some of the major implications of taking joint actions as the basic units of analysis in sociology. We've considered how focusing on joint actions can help shape the broader process of sociological inquiry. As a basis from which to build this general approach to the study of social behavior, we may also consider how this central emphasis on joint actions helps to define, or add meaning to, other familiar concepts in the discipline. Values, status, and networks have been previously discussed; and while examining an exhaustive list of other sociological concepts would be impractical, it may be useful to discuss just a few of them here.

*Patterns of Joint Actions*

## AUTHORITY AND LEADERSHIP

For the successful completion of any joint action, the joint action's plan has to be accepted and followed by the actors involved. Either this is accomplished by mutual discussion and consensus or by the acceptance of some person or persons' authority. The common understandings which are necessary in any joint action have to come from somewhere, and this brings us to the question of sources of authority. And since Max Weber is frequently cited in sociological discussions of authority - charismatic, traditional, and legal-rational - we may make reference to his typology here.

In some joint actions, the participants will accept one person's authority due to their belief that that person has extraordinary capabilities. His or her followers believe that their leader has exceptional intellect, knowledge, physical prowess, skills, or supernatural abilities, and they defer the decision-making process to him or her. We say that the leader has charisma.

Referring to the types of joint actions discussed in Chapter Six, charismatic leaders are most relevant in the partnership and teamwork types. The participants in these joint actions have a common goal, and they believe that "following" this one person is the best way to achieve that goal. It becomes a matter of consensus that the charismatic leader's plan for the joint action will be successful, benefitting all the actors involved.

Charismatic leadership is also common during times of changing circumstances and stress. Changes in the environment, changes in personnel, changes in goals, new opportunities, or threats from others can affect formerly routine activity. When this occurs, existing common understandings and plans may prove to be inadequate for the successful achievement of the actors' goals. In these situations, people will look to someone to devise new or altered plans of action. Charismatic leaders are those people whom their followers trust to come up with successful plans for these circumstances.

Authority based on tradition is most prevalent when certain joint actions have become routine and have persisted across generations. The "tradition" takes the general form, "We've always done things this way, and there is no need to change something that works." Relationships are built on these routine patterns of joint actions, and changes in the routine, or tradition, have a corresponding effect on these relationships. When change occurs, or threatens to occur, people who have held positions of power or privilege will be the first defenders of the status quo, and will do so in the name of tradition. Weber characterized this type of authority as being paternalistic, most likely because, historically, men have held the most power and are most likely to protect existing patterns of interaction in more established, traditional societies.

Legal-rational authority is most prevalent in larger, more complex patterns of joint activity. Large organization's such as corporations, government bodies, and the military engage in these complex joint actions, and they rely heavily on this type of authority.

When patterns of joint actions become complex, there is a greater interdependence among separate joint actions, and there is a greater disconnect between the performance of a given action and the realization of the organization's ultimate goal. In order to maintain stability and coherence in the organization, those in charge establish rules, a code outlining the duties of each "department", and "offices" or "positions", for those people responsible for the successful completion of the different but interdependent joint actions.

The organization thus makes use of a formally constructed rationale for who does what and why. That is, the authority is *rational* because there is a formalized *reason* for the separate joint actions to be performed in a certain way. And this overall formal construction of rules and procedures, and the rationale behind them, ultimately becomes the "legal" source of authority within the organization. Authority does not spring from the inspired ideas of some charismatic leader or from tradition, but comes from a considered logic accepted to be the best way to reach the organization's goals.

## COMMUNITY

To review a bit, self-realization can occur through both task accomplishment and relationship fulfillment during joint actions. When an actor realizes his or her self through relationship fulfillment, the self exists (is defined) as a part of its relationship with one or more others participating in the joint action. When the joint action proceeds as planned, the relationship between the actors becomes "realized". In turn, the actor is able to realize her or his self, and experience the accompanying self satisfaction, by virtue of their being a part of that successful relationship.

This idea of the self being a part of some larger whole (a relationship in a joint action) and being realized as such, can be carried further. People define themselves, and can realize themselves, as part of a larger community. A person becomes a member of a social group by participating in one or more of the group's joint actions. As this participation reoccurs over time, the person comes to identify his or her self more in terms of being a part of this group. The common understandings existing between the actor and the others in the group grow, and all the actors in the group become more "like minded". This facilitates the process of mutual cooperation, and the actors in the group are able to "identify" with one another.

The fact that the members of the group have something in common - that they identify with the group and with one another within the group - gives rise to a sense of community. By participating in the activities of the group, people attain a sense of self worth and self satisfaction as a group member. They are aware of their common identity, and this gives rise to a sense of solidarity with fellow members of their common community. Feelings of self-realization and self satisfaction result from this experience of community with others. And since the group's members' selves become defined as part of this community, they will help defend their community when it is threatened by others. Any threat to the community becomes a threat to themselves.

## Culture

"... Culture is all that in human society which is socially rather than biologically transmitted." (*A Dictionary of Sociology, 1998*) This is perhaps the broadest and most vaguely defined concept in the discipline. In this book's context, and in keeping with the above definition, culture is perhaps best defined as the sum of people's common understandings. That is, culture is the total of what a group of people commonly believe, how they communicate with one another, how they see their world, and how they react to it.

Among the common understandings which comprise a given culture, a common language is the most important. Language consists of the commonly understood meanings of words and gestures. Since words and gestures directly refer to specific objects and actions, language both shapes people's consciousness and enables them to communicate. That is, a language's vocabulary defines and puts limits on the objects that people are aware of and act upon. The sum total of these objects defines the society's world, and this comprises a great part of a society's culture.

In addition to language, culture can refer to all that a given group has in common which separates them from other groups. This, of course, would include a wide range of concepts and phenomena. Styles of appearance, likes and dislikes, and values all contribute to a society's culture. What a group of people commonly understand to be true or not true plays an important role in culture. How people interact, as this interaction differs from the way people interact in other societies, helps define a particular culture. That is, the routines that people follow in a society may follow unique patterns, and this would define a certain characteristic of that society's culture. All these examples are based on the particular common understandings that the people of a given society have and bring into play in their actions. The differences in various societies' cultures stem from the differences in their peoples' common understandings.

This emphasis on common understandings places the concept of culture in close relation to the concept of community. Whereas community designates a particular group of people who interact with one another, culture refers to those common understandings which make this interaction possible and which help the members of the community identify with one another. The study of culture can thus be viewed as the study of those common understandings which define a community. The study of

*Patterns of Joint Actions*

comparative cultures is the study of those common understandings which differ from one community to another.

## Collective Behavior

Collective Behavior may be regarded as a type of joint action in which many people are performing the same action, or actions, at the same time. Examples are political rallies, demonstrations, fans watching and cheering for their favorite team, voting, and mob action.

As the phrase is most typically used, collective behavior refers to people performing these common actions in close proximity to one another. They are able to see and hear one another, and this circumstance tends to reinforce their motivation to action. As they act in concert with one another, they realize that the others are just like themselves, acting and feeling like they are acting and feeling; and this helps justify their own sense of self. They are able to experience a sense of self-realization.

The fact that they are in close proximity to one another, and that the emotions are often highly charged, heightens this feeling of self-realization. They become a living part of something much greater and more intense than themselves. The energy they feel emanating from others reinforces their own emotional experience. This energy and self-realization that they experience also reinforces whatever beliefs, or common understandings, that they hold with one another. That is, the actors' actions are based on a set of beliefs - what they take to be true and not true. By acting in concert, their collective behavior demonstrates to themselves and to anyone watching what these beliefs are. Consequently, collective behavior, in the form of demonstrations and rallies, is a frequent tactic used when people are trying to change other people's minds.

## Personal Networking

Perhaps the most significant and complex consequence of status grouping has to do with networking. When people interact as members of the same status group, it is often in the form of sociable interaction (see Chapter Five). This interaction is generally engaged in for its own sake, supposedly without regard to any business or other outside interests. As people become acquainted via this sociable interaction, they may use this acquaintance to help initiated or further joint actions with one another in other circumstances. The result is a more "close knit" community of people with similar status. The more relationships that people develop with one another, the greater is their network of associations, and the more they may use this network to further other interests such as their business or political careers. Ultimately, as people of higher status become a more closely knit group, political and economic power often become more centralized and more tightly controlled in the hands of a relatively few people.

## "Selflessness"

As discussed in the first chapter, the performance of any action can be broken down into a series of stages:

**(1)** The actor perceives her situation. This is a matter of taking in stimuli from her senses.

**(2)** The actor uses the information she has gathered from her senses to identify the objects around her. She identifies her situation.

**(3)** She considers herself as a part of this situation and notes her place within it. She identifies her feelings, her abilities, wants, and her immediate and long term goals. She establishes her self.

**(4)** Based on her knowledge of the situation and her place within it, she decides which actions to perform. This would include, perhaps, considering a number of different actions and weighing the possible outcomes of each one in order to decide which action will bring her closer to some desired goal.

**(5)** She performs whatever action she has decided is the best one given her assessment of the situation.

*Patterns of Joint Actions*

**(6)** She notes the result of the action, whether or not the action has produced the desired result.

**(7)** She experiences an emotive response depending on the success or failure of the action. With success, she experiences some measure of satisfaction; with failure, she feels some degree of frustration or anger.

A primary goal of Zen is to be "in the moment". It is a matter of maximizing the personal experience by stressing and maximizing the sensual aspects of experience. That which is most *real* to us is that which we can immediately sense and feel. In reference to the above stages of action, it is a matter of getting from stage (1) to stage (7) as quickly and as effortlessly as possible. In the *ideal* Zen state, the actor would sense that which is around her (1) and experience an emotional response (7) simultaneously. This describes being in the moment.

Consequently, a Zen goal is to minimize the effort and time the actor devotes to stages (2) through (6). The less time and effort the actor spends on thinking and deciding, the more she will be "experiencing" the moment. Conversely, the more *problematic* any of these stages are, the more conscious effort the actor has to devote to them. This in turn interferes with the actor's sensual experience. The more thinking an actor has to do prior to acting, the further outside the moment the actor becomes.

The self is prominent in stages (3) and (4) and is often the most problematic feature in the course of performing an action. Being unsure of one's self - being unsure of your abilities, goals, and what others expect of you - can result in considerable reflection, uncertainty, thinking of alternatives, and anxiety on the actor's part, all of which will detract from the actor's experience of the moment. In Oprah Winfrey's words, "There is no moving up and out into the world unless you are fully acquainted with who you are. You cannot move freely, speak freely, act freely, be free unless you are comfortable with yourself." (Newsweek, October 24, 2005)

As a result, achieving a state of "selflessness" becomes crucial to being in the moment. The less a person has to think about himself and consider which action is best to perform, the more immediate will be his response in his situation. By being totally sure of one's self, one becomes essentially oblivious to one's self, or selfless. In such a state, perception, action, and experience become virtually simultaneous - all in the same moment in time.

As an aspect of this selflessness, Zen teachings also stress being in some state of communion or "oneness" with one's surroundings. "Going with the flow" or sensing the unity of oneself with the universe minimizes the sense of self as a separate entity. As one consequence, this attitude stresses an unwillingness to alter or act against one's world. Being at peace with one' surroundings minimizes the need to think, decide, and act; and this maximizes the opportunity to simply experience his surroundings. Here, again, becoming selfless is a means to maximize the actor's personal experience in his world.

Ironically, studying or learning Zen presents something of a conundrum, and this comes to light in some of Zen's more bizarre teachings. Teaching, as a joint action, requires there being a student with an inquiring mind. Students are, by definition, self-conscious and thoughtful. They strive to change from being unknowing to knowing, from being a student to being a master of their subject matter. This typically requires questioning, thought, and reflection; and these processes are at odds with the goals of Zen - they detract from the direct experience of the here and now. Hence, when a student asks a question of a Master, the response is often nonsensical on the surface. Asking and answering involve thinking, and thinking is counterproductive. So the Master's response is often to say something illogical in order to illustrate the futility of searching for some thoughtful, logically correct answer.

# CONCLUSION - APPLICATIONS

● ● ●

SOCIOLOGY'S CHIEF CONTRIBUTION TO CIVILIZATION, in my opinion, has been to stress its basic premise: that for all the differences which exist between peoples, human beings are fundamentally the same - and that their differences stem almost entirely from their different *social* experiences. As significant as this assertion is, it is also a very broad statement. It still leaves an underlying question: What do, or should, sociologists study? In chapter eight, we noted that most sociologists study social groups of one type or another; and we argued that a thorough understanding of any social group should include knowledge of how the group's members interact - either with one another or with members of other groups. Whenever some social group is judged to be distinct from another group, that distinction is best understood in terms of the group's patterns of joint activity and the common understandings that the group's members bring into play. The argument presented here is that a viable, and often complementary, alternative to focusing on social groups is to focus on joint actions as primary units of research and analysis.

It remains to be seen just how the concepts and theories of sociologists will evolve. The *pragmatic* view is that the ideas that persist will be the ones that *work*. Ideas and theories are tools - tools which people use to help solve problems and achieve goals. Ideas tend to be accepted as fact if they prove reliable and useful in reaching goals. They need to find applications in the real world.

Will a focus on the fundamentals of social interaction prove to have value in the real world? For one thing, having a knowledge and sensitivity as to how and why joint actions succeed or fail, I believe, can go a long way in addressing and finding solutions to many social problems. All social interaction is, at least potentially, problematic. When looking at social problems, a number of questions may be addressed. What joint actions are the people who are involved in these problems engaged in? What are their *goals*? Do these have a viable and realistic *plan* to reach those goals? Are their *common understandings* truly common and realistically based on the facts of the situation? Are they able to *communicate* effectively and adapt to changing circumstances? Are ongoing *patterns* of joint activity being sustained, or are they changing? Are the actors achieving their individual goals? Are they completing their individual tasks and fulfilling their relationships - are they achieving *self-realization*? Do their efforts to achieve self-realization come into conflict with other people's routines and careers? As their actions alter the situation, will any changes made affect the overall environment?

Such a list of questions, as an example, may be applied to an analysis of large organizations in seeking to find out how effectively they operate. Any weakness in an organization may be attributed to a problem in one or more of the areas cited above. And once these problems are isolated and examined, certain realistic solutions may become more readily apparent. As time goes by, analyses following this general approach may become more formalized and perhaps find purchase in the real world.

# REFERENCES

Becker, Howard (1974). *Outsiders: Studies in the Sociology of Deviance*. New York, New York: The Free Press.

Blau, Peter (1994). *Structural Contexts of Opportunities*. Chicago, Illinois: The University of Chicago Press.

Blumer, Herbert (1954). "What is wrong with Social Theory?", *The American Sociological Review*, Vol. XIX. The American Sociological Association.

Blumer, Herbert (1966). "Sociological Implications of the Thought of George Herbert Mead", *The American Journal of Sociology*, LXXI, pp.535-544. Chicago, Illinois: The University of Chicago Press.

Blumer, Herbert (1969). *Symbolic Interactionism, Perspective and Method*. Englewood Cliffs, New Jersey: Prentice Hall.

Cooley, Charles Horton (1902). *Human Nature and Social Order*. New York, New York: Scribner.

Denzin, Norman (1969). "The Methodologies of Symbolic Interaction: A Critical Review of Research Techniques" from *Social Psychology Through Symbolic Interaction* (Stone and Farberman, eds.). Waltham Massachusetts: Ginn-Blaisdell.

Denzin, Norman K. (1970). *The Research Act: A Theoretical Introduction to Sociological Methods*. Aldine Publishing Co., Chicago, Illinois.

Goffman, E. (1959). *The Presentation of Self in Everyday Life*. Garden City, New York: Doubleday.

Homans, George C. (1958). "Social Behavior as Exchange" *The American Journal of Sociology*, 63:6 pp. 597-606. Chicago, Illinois: The University of Chicago Press.

Lindesmith A., Strauss, A., & Denzin, N. (1999) *Social Psychology.* Thousand Oaks, CA: Sage Publications.

Marshall, Gordon (ed.). *A Dictionary of Sociology* (1998). Oxford, England: Oxford University Press.

Mills, C. Wright (1956). *The Power Elite.* New York: Oxford University Press.

Parsons, Talcott (1949). *The Structure of Social Action.* Glencoe, Illinois: Free Press.

Scheff, T. J. (1967). "Toward a Sociological Model of Consensus" *The American Sociological Review*, XXXII, #1, pp. 32-46. The American Sociological Association.

Simmel, Georg (1971). *On Individuality and Social Forms.* Donald N. Levine (ed.), Chicago, Illinois: The University of Chicago Press.

Veblen, Thorsten (1899). *The Theory of the Leisure Class.* New York, New York: Penguin Books.

Made in the USA
Charleston, SC
08 February 2017